GET IT DNE

THE 21-DAY MIND HACK SYSTEM
TO DOUBLE YOUR PRODUCTIVITY
AND FINISH WHAT YOU START

MICHAEL MACKINTOSH

TCK PUBLISHING.COM

CONTENTS

INTRODUCTION

"Most of us have two lives. The life we live, and the unlived life within us. Between the two stands Resistance."

— STEVEN PRESSFIELD

WHO THIS BOOK IS FOR

This book is for creative entrepreneurs who have a mission and a message to deliver to the world. I call them Awakened Creators, people who have chosen to awaken their genius and use their gifts to do meaningful work in the world.

Bringing our ideas to life isn't easy and too often we find ourselves stalling, procrastinating, or holding back. Sure, we have an endless list of excuses for why we do this and a lot of them are completely legitimate—we're burned out, we're working all the time, we have too many obligations, and on and on. But, deep down, we know we could be much farther along in our work than we are now *if only we would just do what we need to do*. We're not getting the results we want, and yet we keep putting off the important things we know we need to do.

Sound familiar?

This Book Is for You If...

- You want to have more freedom, more income, and more impact
- You're under-achieving and under-delivering
- You're tired of your own excuses
- You're ready to stop holding back
- You have something important inside you to share with the world
- You're ready for a change and are willing to do what it takes

And most important....

You're up for the challenge!

THE BIG PROMISE

I believe you can be at least 2-16 times more successful than you currently are. All you'll need to make this upgrade is to show up fully in your power, stay focused on your most impactful project, and stop wasting time on the small stuff that's getting you nowhere.

You are extremely powerful. You have a message to share and many lives to change. Once you get those annoying negative voices out of your head, shed those ineffective working habits, and overcome your reasons for playing small instead of big, I know you'll be free to create fearlessly and make amazing things happen. And you'll be able to do it *fast*.

Today Can Be the Day That Everything Changes for You

This book is designed to get you the results you want in both your business and your life. You will discover the tools and mindset you'll need to take massive action and bring your ideas to life in 21 days or less.

By Reading and Applying the Principles You're About to Learn, You'll Be Able To:

1. Finish projects you've started but stalled on

2. Start projects you've been putting off 'til that perfect moment (that never comes)

3. "Ship" your work (get it out of your head, off your laptop, and into the world where it's meant to be)

4. Make more money (by actually doing the things that create wealth)

5. Be at least twice as productive as you are now...

...in 21 Days...or less.

As a Pleasant Side Effect of Reading This, You'll Also Be Able To:

1. Have more time off to relax, rejuvenate, and feel inspired

2. Think clearly and calmly about what's important and break free from the cycle of constantly "putting out fires"

3. End old dysfunctional relationships that no longer serve you

Perhaps best of all, you'll be able to apply these same methods to almost any area of your life: your health, relationships, spirituality, and hobbies. And, you'll be able create the new habits you want or need to live your dream life.

I know, so many great sounding ideas and claims fail miserably. This is different. What you are about to learn are not just nice ideas that won't make any difference in real life. No, these are practical, proven tools and techniques that I've gleaned from great leaders who've used them to turn their ideas into fortunes.

By applying the same principles I'm sharing here in my own life, I've experienced what can only be called miracles. I've gone from being the chronic procrastinator everyone thought would end up on government benefits and drinking beer all day to an international spiritual teacher, a best-selling author of multiple books, creator of 15 courses and training programs, and the cofounder of OmBar Chocolate Company. I've done all this while enjoying a relaxing, beautiful life on the paradise island of Kauai and in sunny Sedona with the love of my life.

It's fair to say these ideas really work—not just for me, but also for the thousands of students who've applied them.

To make the great shift and turn our lives around, we need to break free from the lethal habits of procrastination, perfectionism, stalling, over-thinking, and getting distracted in low-value activities that don't do anything to improve our lives.

As long as procrastination has you in its iron grip, you'll never be able to achieve your biggest dreams and goals in life. You'll keep putting off things that matter most to you and continue to get mediocre results. Worst of all, you'll keep waking up tired and uninspired.

You have too much awesomeness to experience! In 21 days, you can create miracles, or you can stay stuck where you are. Those 21 days will pass no matter what, so it's up to you where you want to be at the end of them.

If you're ready to give procrastination a damn good whack in the head, get your most important work in life done, and make the income and impact you deserve, then let's get started.

WHY THIS BOOK IS DIFFERENT

There are countless motivational books that may inspire you to share your gifts and live the life you love. The problem with most of these books is they forget to include a proven method to overcome the Resistance that holds so many back. Many books may inspire you to act, but they don't tell you *how* to do it consistently and reliably.

It's like the salesman who drives to work every day listening to motivational talks, pumped with coffee and inspiration to take on the day. But come 5:00, he's back at the bar surrounded by other deflated, depressed souls grumbling about their bad luck.

Or the excited author-to-be who wakes up in the morning, checks her phone in hope of some new inspiration, and then spends the rest of her day on social media or doing "research" online. By the end of the day she hasn't written a single word of her book.

These people don't lack motivation or inspiration. What they are missing is a proven system to take their ideas and use them to create the results they want. Motivation is essential, *but it's not enough.*

I wrote this book to give you the step-by-step system for taking your big ideas and bringing them to life quickly and consistently. The more you use and refine this system for yourself, the more powerful it becomes and the better your life will turn out.

You may know where you want to go in your life and work; this method is like a jet plane to get you there as quickly as possible. Now, instead of just dreaming and hoping, every day you wake up closer and closer to your heart's true desires. Every day you take leaps and bounds directly into your new great life. Instead of having an unlived life inside you, today is the beginning of your life becoming the life you were meant to live.

HOW THIS BOOK WORKS

What you have in this book is access to a powerful, proven system to radically increase your results. The Get It Done 21 Day Challenge is your opportunity to take an idea you have in your mind and bring it to life in 21 days. For most people, months and years fly past with little or no significant impact. It's the same old, same old, over and over and over, and nothing much changes.

With this 21 day challenge, you can turn your life into an adventure. Or, more accurately, if you consistently follow these steps you will turn your life into a series of little 21 day adventures that will bring your full power to each project so you can finally make big leaps forward in life. This means that by the end of a year, you'll be so radically ahead of where you are now you'll feel as if you're living in another world entirely.

Once you get started using these tools, every day will be meaningful, and you'll have crystal clear focus on what matters most to you. Every day will be an opportunity to move quickly and effectively toward your goals and dreams. Even better, the more you do this, the better you will feel about yourself and your life. Every day that you succeed, your confidence increases and inspires you to do more and make the next day even better. Integrating these principles of successful action will replace vicious cycles of stagnation with virtuous cycles of success, fun, magic, wealth, wonder, and impact.

Your new level of focus combined with the system you're about to learn will transform you from someone who is living at only about 10% of their potential into someone who can achieve almost anything you put your mind to. It's like going from driving a broken down old car that rattles and squeaks into one that flies at super-fast jet speeds of over 2,000 MPH. You may not want to fly quite that fast, but it's good to know you can if you want to!

For best results, before you officially start your first 21 day challenge, read this book all the way through so you fully understand the basics. Then start your first 21 day challenge using the worksheets in this book as your guide.

THIS BOOK IS DIVIDED INTO THREE PARTS

Part I: The 11 Essential Mind Hacks to Become a Super-Charged Action-Taker

In Part 1, you'll discover the 11 most important mindsets and insights you need to bring your ideas powerfully into life in a short time. These mindsets allow you to see life from a new perspective, which in turn will allow you to act differently.

Part II: The Get It Done 21 Day Challenge

In Part 2, you'll learn the how to do the Get It Done 21 Day Challenge, the unstoppable system that guarantees you'll finish projects in record time. It's a step-by-step system that destroys crippling Resistance and procrastination and allows you to finish what you start. This system is proven to work, but if you want to make it work for you, you need to actually use it and not skip steps. Once you get used to it, you'll wonder how you ever managed without it and it will become second nature.

vi

Part III: Start Your 21 Day Challenge

And finally, there comes a time when theory has to end and action must begin. In Part 3, everything comes together, and you set yourself up for your first 21 day challenge. This is where all the insights and understanding you've gained become practical and you get started on your first adventure to greatness. To make this easy for you, I've also included additional online resources, videos, audio, and other tools to help you do your 21 day challenge and succeed. All these bonuses are offered to you for free as part of this book. Make sure you access them in Part III.

Once you've done your first 21 day challenge, you can go back and do another and another and another, each time compounding success upon success until you become unstoppable.

At the very end of the book, you'll find a quick reference sheet that covers the most important things to keep in mind as you do your 21 day challenge. Use this to help keep you on track.

Take your time to get familiar with the ideas and fully understand all the principles outlined in this book. Each principle you understand and apply will help you improve your life one meaningful step at a time.

THANK YOU FOR BEING HERE

I want you to know that I have an enormous amount of respect for you. I believe in you. I'm excited about the wonders you can create with your life and all the good you can do in the world.

I'm not going to pander to your ego or play nice to the part of you that's holding you back, though. That part of you that wants to play small and waste your time repeating your past is about to get with the program and start repeating success after success.

YOUR ESSENTIAL BONUS TO GET MORE DONE & HAVE MORE FUN!

"THE GET IT DONE MASTERS PROGRAM" (VALUE $385)

Want to make your success easier? Included with your purchase of this book are powerful additional resources to supercharge your productivity, destroy Resistance, and make things happen.

By using this book along with these complimentary, step-by-step resources, you are making your success inevitable.

Your 21 Day Challenge Productivity Super Charge includes:

- A step-by-step video instruction guide on how to set up your 21 day challenge
- Powerful resources to explode your creativity and enable you to think more clearly
- Real methods to overcome Resistance, self-sabotage, and creative blocks for good
- Bonus resources to double your productivity and get more done with less effort

Plus you'll also discover:

- How to take more time off, have more fun, and enjoy yourself (this is essential for you to be productive and have an enjoyable, meaningful life)
- How to celebrate your success and love your life
- Guided meditations to make you more relaxed, more creative, and think more clearly
- Additional recommended reading
- And a lot more

Make sure you get access to this wealth of invaluable resources for FREE in Part III of the book.

PART I

11 ESSENTIAL MIND HACKS TO MAKE THINGS HAPPEN

CHAPTER 1

ESSENTIAL MIND HACK #1

THE PROLONGED PAIN OR THE SHORT-LIVED PAIN

"Pain in life is inevitable but suffering is not."

— BUDDHA

Over the years, we've been fed all kinds of nonsensical ideas about life and what it takes to make things happen. Many of these ideas are simply false and subtly sabotage our ability to act and become successful. That's why we need new insights to see clearly and be able to make things happen. Once you know these mindsets, you'll stop seeing the world in a deluded way that prevents you from moving forward. As you'll soon realize, the way the world appears to us is not always the way the world really is. Rewiring our minds for success is not only a good strategy, it's absolutely necessary.

We've been lied to about what it takes to be successful. We've been led to believe that anyone and everyone can be successful, that success should be easy and fast. The truth is life is wonderful, but it's also painful. Pain comes to everyone at some point and takes many forms. How pain affects us and how we respond to it is up to us. What is certain is that we can't avoid pain.

Unfortunately, we're fed the big myth that we can have everything we want without getting out of our comfort zone or experiencing any challenges. These ideas leave most people with absurd expectations that eventually make them feel disillusioned and angry.

Having spent the last 20-plus years working with people from all over the world, I've seen these myths emerge over and over again. The fantasy persists that simply by taking a course or buying a book a person can be magically transformed into a vastly superior version of themselves and their entire life will radically improve. The (unconscious) idea is that once we know about something, we can carry on as before doing all the same old things, and yet somehow get radically better results. In other words, people are taught and then believe that they can stay the same as they are and yet improve their entire lives. No one will openly admit to this, but it's nevertheless going on all the time in the backs of their minds, preventing them from actually creating the success they want.

The truth about life is that it isn't as sexy as the fantasy story we've read. But when you embrace the truth and see life as it really is, your life becomes a magical adventure. Changing your life and bringing ideas to life isn't easy. If it were, you'd already have done it and you'd have everything you want in life. But you haven't...and that's why you're reading this book.

If we're willing to be completely honest, we'll see that real, lasting, positive change is actually quite rare and not easy to achieve. This is why so few people are successful and so many people live unfulfilled, unsuccessful lives. Most people say they want to change, but as the years go by, they don't. Why not? Why do so few people really get ahead in life and achieve their dreams? Change is challenging because as we wrench ourselves away from an old familiar habit and begin forming a new one, we often feel stressed, confused, overwhelmed, and disoriented.

As we change things in our lives, we face unfamiliar territory and new types of challenges that are uncomfortable for us. So to avoid feeling awkward, most people give up too soon and revert to the bad habits they're used to, even though those habits do not make them happy. At least it's the devil they know, right? Change isn't easy; if you look at your own attempts to bring about change, I'm sure you'll agree.

But it's not that simple...***not changing your life isn't easy either!***

While change is hard, feeling stuck and wading around in tedious BS that doesn't get you anywhere has its own set of challenges. Every day that we put off doing what we need to do and live below our potential we die a little. Each day we waste, we feel a little more depressed, apathetic, and lost. When we're limiting ourselves, we feel something is wrong with our lives and we slowly slip backward while our life passes by without meaning or happiness.

Either way, whether we choose to change and improve ourselves or choose to stay stuck, life isn't easy. And either way, we will still experience some kind of pain.

So, there it is: the raw, honest truth most people want to ignore. Life isn't easy, and, one way or another, we're going to feel at least some degree of discomfort or pain. Challenges will come to every one of us, even if we try to avoid them. No matter how successful we are, or how much money we have, we'll all experience some kind of pain in our lives.

You know this already. Now the billion-dollar question is: will we take the *long pain* or the *short pain?*

Will you choose to play small and avoid the pain of change? Or will you face it head on and get it over and done with?

Will you choose the comfortable path you know? Or will you choose the uncharted path you don't?

THE LONG PAIN OF AN UNLIVED LIFE

When we take the long pain, we are trying to avoid immediate discomfort in our lives by distracting ourselves and settling for less than what we are capable of achieving. Choosing the long pain means running from pain in the short term but ending up depressed and neurotic because we haven't fulfilled our life's mission.

According to Carl Jung, "Neurosis is a life designed around avoiding authentic suffering." This is exactly what happens when we take the long pain. Most of us assume we are terrified of death, but we're really just afraid of living. We're petrified of life. So we avoid living authentically. We avoid having the hard conversations with those close to us because doing so will cause short-term discomfort. The consequence is that we put up with dysfunctional relationships for years, even decades. We avoid finishing our projects because we're afraid someone may not approve of us, and by doing so we rob ourselves of the possibility of success and fulfillment. When we take the long pain, we avoid doing what we need to do to achieve our potential, often in every aspect of our lives. Instead, we play small and live shadow lives of quiet desperation.

This is an unhappy, frustrating, and deadly place to exist. From a mythical perspective, taking the long pain means that the hero is hiding in a cave sleeping all day instead of going out and slaying the dragons and claiming the treasures—all while his kingdom is being slaughtered.

Procrastination is a sure sign of taking the long pain. It is often seen as a sign of laziness, but it's not—it's simply a way to avoid the short pain. Perfectionism, making excuses, and wasting time in constant stress and crisis that never ends are all ways of taking (and accepting) the long pain instead of enduring the short pain.

When we take the long pain and live an inauthentic life, our lives revolve around avoiding what's most important. We don't want to feel authentic suffering. We don't feel fully alive so we hide from ourselves by wasting our days choosing easier and less painful alternatives that ultimately lead to a slow, sad, and dissatisfying life of misery.

Some Signs of Choosing the Prolonged Pain Are:

- Excessively checking your cell phone, emails, messages, alerts, and notifications
- Living in a state of constant crisis (or busyness) without enough time to think clearly about what's truly important
- Complaining and blaming others
- Being passive-aggressive
- Excessive interest in entertainment, drugs, or other distractions
- Knowing you should change something in your life but staying with it anyway out of fear or familiarity
- Spending more time on social media than actually doing the work
- Addictions of all kinds
- Enduring toxic relationships

When we're taking the long pain, as soon as a thought or feeling surfaces to make us aware that we need to do something truly important, we go unconscious and distract ourselves with getting something to eat, something to drink, and doing the things we're comfortable doing.

We try to avoid short-term pain and having to face ourselves through procrastination, perfectionism, distraction, and crisis management. But all this avoidance leads us to something far more terrifying—a life of chronic low-level depression, boredom, misery, and a deep sense of dissatisfaction.

By avoiding pain in the moment, we constantly feel restless and deny ourselves an authentic life. By avoiding authentic suffering, we settle for a sedated half-life and deny ourselves the true satisfaction and richness of living our true purpose.

Procrastination and taking the long pain means choosing the long, grueling, self-created gnawing pain of an unlived, sad life that you try to blame on others, but deep down you know it's your own fault. The long pain is where we try to live life the easy way by taking pills, distracting ourselves, sedating ourselves, and chasing cheap thrills. We all know this doesn't work. Soon enough, we're left feeling sick and depleted again.

Procrastination is our way of dealing with problems through avoidance and distraction. We hope that if we just ignore them, things will somehow go away. But, the problems are just sitting outside your front door waiting for you to come out. The consequence of living the easy way and taking the long pain is that we end up trapped in a messy, stressful, unsuccessful life that's full of crisis, drama, debt, and chronic fear. It's a life of slavery: a cruel curse that we have inflicted on ourselves.

The Long Pain Will Be Infinitely Worse and More Painful Than the Short Pain

The good news is we can radically reduce our suffering and increase our pleasure if we're willing to face ourselves, face our lives, and choose the short pain over the long pain.

THE SHORT PAIN

To choose the short pain means to live an authentic, meaningful life. It means we face the things that no longer serve us, deal with the challenges they bring, and create transformation even though it's temporarily uncomfortable. Taking the short pain gives us a meaningful life of authentic suffering that leads to joy, freedom, wealth, love, and deep satisfaction.

The short pain is where we bite the bullet and face our problems. We get a quick shock that feels terrible for a moment but swiftly fades away and transforms into profound lightness, freedom, joy, and excitement. By taking the short pain, we choose to face our challenges *today* so we can avoid recurring pain in the future. The short pain is when you face up to and resist the craving for junk food that's tasty but making you sick—so you go without it to experience long-term energy and health. The short pain might be ending a relationship that's going nowhere and thereby avoiding years of misery and arguments so that you can have an open heart for the relationship of true love you've always wanted.

Remember This Statement from Marketer Joe Polish:

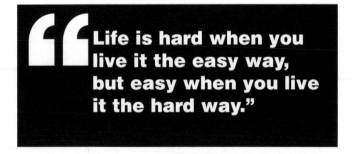

"Life is hard when you live it the easy way, but easy when you live it the hard way."

When I first heard this at a conference, it hit me between the eyes and smashed the deluded comfort seeker who had been driving the bus of my life. Since then, my life has never been the same.

Here is why: at every moment, you can choose to be tempted with little pleasures that lead to a hard life of endless crisis and tedious BS, or you can face the music now and create a life of long-lasting ease, grace, freedom, health, wealth, and happiness.

Check in with yourself.

- Do you truly realize you can't avoid all forms of pain forever?
- Are you ready to face the authentic pain that comes from doing what you need to do?
- Are you excited to face your fears and get back to work on your life's mission?

The good news is right now you have the power to reduce (or increase) the amount of pain in your life by choosing the long pain or the short pain. Right now you can end long-term misery simply by choosing to do what you need to do.

WHAT'S YOUR CHOICE: THE LONG PAIN OR THE SHORT PAIN?

Life is definitely going to bring various forms of pain to each of us. No matter how hard we try, we can never completely avoid pain. If that comes as a shock to you, sorry, but living a 100% pain-free, drama-free life is simply not possible. Maybe at some other point in our human journey this will be possible, but not right now. Even if we had all the money and facilities in the world to try to avoid pain throughout our lives, we could still get sick, feel worried or stressed, get angry, or be hungry, depressed, or lonely. Avoiding life and playing small is painful. Living with unfinished projects is painful. We can't escape pain. So trying to avoid all forms of pain is both impossible and pointless. It leads to a life of neurosis and emptiness.

Let's do ourselves a favor, give up the delusion, and get on our mission!

CHAPTER 2

ESSENTIAL MIND HACK #2

THE DEFINING CHOICE

Right now you can choose to re-create your past and continue doing the same things you've always done, or you can start creating a brand new future and create the things you desire in your life. One year from today, you can either be pretty much where you are now or you can be living your dreams. Today can be the day everything changes forever.

We don't wake up every morning, stand before the mirror, and say to ourselves, "Today, I'm going to repeat the same old stupid, self-defeating, destructive habits that made me miserable yesterday." But so often that's exactly what we do. Day in and day out, it's the same old, same old BS that has led us to where we are. If we want to *really* make a shift, we need to abandon the stuff that has not been working and do something else. We can't just do the same things over and over and expect different results. We know this, but knowing it intellectually is not enough. It's time we did something about it. It's time to really change.

The good news is we have the ability to change. We can become self-aware, recognize the state of our existence, and choose to change ourselves and our behavior. We can re-create ourselves. We can retrain ourselves. We can make little shifts to our thinking and actions that lead to massive long-term results in our lives. We can, in a sense, re-create ourselves and be reborn many times within one life. We can choose to start over. Even if you've failed before, you can choose to create a new life for yourself. And it can happen quickly. You just need to want it enough.

CHANGE IS A CHOICE

You have to act differently and think differently to get different results. While this may sound blatantly obvious, it hasn't hit home for most people. Right now, the vast majority of the human population seems to think they *can* do the same old thing and get a different result. Just look around. Most people do the same things over and over every day, refusing to change and yet expecting a different result, hoping things will somehow, miraculously, turn out better. Seriously, look around and see for yourself. Look at your own life. Look at the last six months. Look at the last 10 years.

Massive changes happen when we choose to take massive action in a new way. We can choose to make that shift anytime we want. For most of us, the big changes never happen unless a serious problem forces us to wake up and do something different.

That magic moment can happen now. It can happen *right now.*

Do you want to carry on doing the same things and expecting a different result? Or are you willing to become part of the 1% who make the great leap and actually get a different result?

Today is your big day. Today can be the day your whole life changes. You have all you need to do it. But you first need to be willing to be a little bit uncomfortable and do the stuff you need to do.

If you want to make something happen, you don't need another book. You don't need more theory, case studies, clever graphics, charts, or motivational speakers. You need to stop screwing around and start getting it done. You need to apply systems and strategies that work so procrastination doesn't stand a chance against you. It all starts right here, right now, with your willingness to become an action taker.

It starts with a choice.

Are you willing to upgrade the way you think and act so you can create better results in your life?

HERE ARE A FEW QUESTIONS TO DETERMINE HOW SERIOUS *YOU REALLY ARE* ABOUT MAKING THINGS HAPPEN

Really tune into to these questions and feel your response.

1. Are you willing to be successful and wealthy?

2. Are you willing to become someone who takes massive action and gets massive results?

3. Are you willing to give up distracting yourself and procrastinating with pointless entertainment and random time wasting?

4. Are you willing to stop doing things that don't generate results?

5. Are you willing to make TODAY the day you become a hard-core action taker and make things happen?

6. Are you willing to stop being the old "me" and become a new "me," an upgraded version of who you are?

How do you feel about this? If you have any resistance, that's okay. Just ask the questions again until you get clear, because if you're not willing to change, then what's the point in reading this book?

If you're not freaked out by this then you're probably not being fully present with these questions. If you get it, you'll feel some serious emotions like fear, worry, or doubt. Fear (and excitement) is a sign that change is beginning to stir within you.

IF YOU'RE NOT FEELING IT, RE-READ THE QUESTIONS UNTIL YOU FEEL UNCOMFORTABLE *AND* EXCITED

You need to become "not me" to make this shift. You need to begin to see that old version of you, the one who can't get it done, as someone who needs to retire so that the massive action-taker within you can take charge and make it happen. Are you willing to let that old self, that old identity be replaced and upgraded? Are you willing to go to the edge of your comfort zone and create profound breakthroughs? Are you willing to become an upgraded version of yourself?

You have a vast store of untapped power waiting to be released. You know it's there; you can probably feel it. And the first step to awaken the power within is simply to be willing to change. Willingness is the key to transformation. When you take one step of courage you receive one thousand steps of support. When you're willing to become someone who makes things happen, we can move on.

Remember this defining moment can happen anytime. It doesn't have to be a once-in-a-lifetime experience. You can choose to let go of the limited past and open yourself to new experiences and new ways of being anytime you wish. Life can be magical and fun if you want. You can take a daring new step in a better direction now. You can make today the best day of your life—if you want.

Are you willing to become the highest version of yourself?

ESSENTIAL MIND HACK #3

THE 80/20 RULE

You may already know about the 80/20 rule, but in case you've never heard of it, the 80/20 rule, also known as the Pareto Principle and the Law of the Vital Few, is a power law named after the Italian economist, Vilfredo Pareto.

This "law" states that approximately 80% of inputs (causes) lead to a mere 20% of outputs (results) while just 20% of inputs or causes lead to a whopping 80% of results. In other words, **the 80/20 rule says that *just a few things in life matter a lot* while the rest is essentially pointless and trivial.** Once we "get" this revolutionary discovery, our mission is to discover what those few things are and do more of them while doing less of the rest.

Pareto discovered this law while studying wealth distribution in Italy. He found that approximately 80% of the land was owned by less than 20% of the population. Finding this curious, he conducted several other surveys on land ownership and wealth distribution in other countries over different periods of time. To his astonishment, he found a similar 80/20 relationship held true in all countries and in all time periods he studied.

Wherever he looked he found that a few people had most of the land and wealth while the majority of people had to make do with the rest. The same holds true today. A small minority of super rich still hold most of the wealth while the majority is left with the rest. Pareto finally developed the 80/20 principle after observing his garden and discovering the 80/20 relationship at work there as well: 20% of the pea pods contained 80% of the peas.

SO WHAT DO PEA PODS AND THE 80/20 RULE HAVE TO DO WITH YOU?

Everything. The 80/20 rule means that a few things you do each day (about 20% of your actions) get you 80% of your results and have a significantly positive impact on your life overall. So most (80%) of what you do is essentially a waste of time. Or, 80% of what you do all day long is total BS. Take this in for a moment.

This law says most of what we do every day is BS, and only a few things really matter. Once you realize this, you'll want to pay close attention to what the good stuff is and what's simply frivolous time-wasting disguised as work.

For example, if you worked for 10 hours, two of those hours would lead to 80% of the results you achieved for that day—the good stuff. The other eight hours would only create 20% of the impact. That means you will have spent eight hours working and being busy without any significant results to show for it.

SO WHY NOT GO TO THE BEACH FOR THOSE EIGHT HOURS AND STOP SCREWING AROUND PRETENDING TO BE BUSY?

This is such a shocking revelation that it needs to be said again.

Just a few things you do each day (20% or less) are having an amazingly positive impact on your life (producing 80% of your results), while most of what you do (80% of your time) is essentially a waste of energy and has only a marginally positive impact on your life (20% impact). In fact, some of the things you've been doing make no impact at all or even make your life worse!

This means just a few things you do each day keep your life going well while the rest could be removed, and you'd still be fine. So, if you want to be a ninja instead of running around each day like a headless chicken, you'll identify your top 20% activities—and then do more of them.

Practically speaking, this means in a 10-hour day, only two hours are really getting you anywhere.

So once you know what the "good 20%" is, you can duplicate it. Now, with just four hours of work you could get a 160% increase in results, and have six extra hours to do anything you want.

Would you rather be more productive and have more time off? Or would you prefer keeping your nose to the grindstone and wasting your life wading about in a truckload of turds?

It's your call.

Many people know this intellectually, but they don't act on it. Instead they simply carry on wasting their precious life in low value work and wonder why "success" never comes.

The good news is you can do LESS and get a better result if you're smart and figure out what the good stuff is and do more of it every day. This will take a little bit of hard thinking to avoid countless days, months, and years of hard work and floundering around. What's even cooler is that this bizarre ratio applies to every aspect of our lives.

Here are just a few examples to get you thinking...

YOUR RELATIONSHIPS

Right now, approximately 20% of your relationships bring you about 80% of your joy, while the other 80% only have a small impact on your life. On the other side, another 20% of your relationships will be the cause of 80% of your *unhappiness*.

Who are the top people who bring you the most joy? How can you spend more time with them?

Who are the other people who screw up your life? How can you spend less time with them, or make those relationships work?

When you know the answers to these questions you can swiftly increase your level of happiness and remove your stress. Is it worth it? You bet it is.

YOUR FOOD AND DRINK

Approximately 20% of your food and drink choices bring you about 80% of your health, while the other 80% only has a mild impact on your life and health.

On the other side, about 20% of the "bad" or unhealthy food you eat is probably what's making you fat, sick, and ugly. So if you give that up, you'll feel a lot better.

You probably also eat the same 20% of foods 80% of the time. Right now I'm drinking coffee. I drink coffee about 80% of the time for my morning session and have other drinks about 20% of the time.

Certain foods and drinks promote better focus and energy, allowing you to be more focused when you have important work to do. Ginseng and other adaptogenic herbs (rhodiola, chaga, reishi, astragalus, ashwagandha, marine phytoplankton, and many more) all have long track records of helping people gain better balance in their lives in a holistic way. You don't need to do them all. Find what works for you and do that.

There are plenty of studies showing that adding raw, plant-based foods to our daily diet brings us more overall health and staves off disease.

Start by adding the good stuff instead of taking away... the bad things will fall away in time. You will enjoy better sleep, vitality, focus, and energy. It is well worth your while to integrate these beneficial lifestyle choices into your daily rituals for short and long-term results.

YOUR WORK AND MONEY

Approximately 20% of your work activities bring you about 80% of your income, while the other 80% only have a small impact on your cash flow (and may even cost you money). So if you simply focus on that 20% you'll make more money.

If you want to try to do everything, you might end up wading about in that truckload of BS that gets you nowhere.

PLACES YOU TRAVEL

You probably go to the same places for work and play 80% of the time and other places about 20% of the time.

Are you going to the coolest spots? Or are you going to places that are "okay" but not really doing it for you? Why not find the places you most love to go to and go there more often? Where else could you travel to that would bring you more joy and take about the same time to get to?

MOVIES AND ENTERTAINMENT

What types of movies do you enjoy (or actors do you like)? How can you watch more inspiring movies? Or give up movies altogether and do something else!

The 80/20 rule applies to everything else you do, including:

- Emails sent to you and emails you send to others
- Clothes you wear
- Stuff you buy
- The quality of your spiritual practices
- The books or types of books you read
- And the list goes on...

If you go to your local health food shop, you'll see the same people there 80% of the time buying their "healthy" food. If you were to look at the store's accounting, you'd see that about 80% of their sales will come from 20% of the customers, and 20% of the products will make up 80% of the sales.

Many companies are profitable because they focus on the top 20% of the products and services that people want and reduce or scrap the rest.

If you look into it enough, you'll find this "rule of the vital few" in operation over and over again in every area of your life. It may not be an exact 80/20 relationship, but it will be close. Maybe it's more like 90/10 or 70/30, but the point is that a few things are having a big impact on your life and the rest are taking up most of your time and only giving you back a tiny return.

That meager 20% of things you do are not just a little bit better than the remaining 80%. They are, on average, 16 times more effective than the other 80%.

THE GOOD STUFF IS 16X BETTER THAN THE BAD STUFF

Has your jaw dropped? Are you awestruck, unable to speak or move? If not, you haven't understood this yet. Go back and read this again until it hits you. Knowing and applying this will RADICALLY upgrade the quality of your life. Right now, 80% of what you do is a waste of time and can be removed or dramatically reduced.

I'll say this again.

80% of what you do with your time is equivalent to wading about in a truckload of manure.

20% of what you do is keeping your life together. If you did more of this 20%, you'd radically improve the quality of your results (and your life).

So now you have a choice about how you work and what you do. Will you choose Option A or Option B?

OPTION A – THE 80% BS METHOD

The 80% BS Method is like dragging a bull up a hill for six hours and then spending the rest of the day rolling about in his feces and *paying* for the privilege.

OPTION B – THE 20% EASY SUCCESS METHOD

The 20% Easy Success Method is like flying a private jet plane at 800 miles an hour to a private island to relax while you make money on autopilot.

Which would you prefer?

If this 80/20 thing doesn't strike you as astounding and revolutionary, you haven't fully understood it yet. Seriously. If a light has been turned on and this principle has registered with you, you should be in a state of awe and excitement right now.

You'll have the big Aha! moment and realize that you've been wasting 80% of your time and you could be claiming it back by using that time to do more of the things that matter most and produce the greatest beneficial impact in your life.

If the light is on, you've just discovered the keys to your freedom. You now have to use this key if you want to unlock the door to your success. When my clients "get it," they become amazed and eager to start discovering the good 20% and increasing it in their lives.

Knowing this law of life is like being given a magic key to a new reality where you can enjoy life, work less, and make a bigger impact. It's like having a whole new world you never knew existed suddenly open up to you. You're awakening from a nightmare and creating a dream in which you have control over what happens. Awesome as it is though, it takes courage to stop doing the 80% BS and focus on the gold.

Do you have the courage to change? Are you willing to stop the BS? Are you willing to get it together? Now is the moment of power.

Cut out the low-value, unproductive things you've been doing and claim back your life. With just this one essential mindset shift you can double your productivity overnight.

CHAPTER 4

ESSENTIAL MIND HACK #4

GOOD IS GOOD ENOUGH

Dan Sullivan wrote about a great approach to life for creative people that helps make sure you don't get stuck trying to be a perfectionist.

Sullivan's approach focuses on the power of getting most of the way to success, say 90% of the way to perfect, and not worrying about attempting to go all the way to 100%, which is impossible, extremely time consuming, and in most cases, entirely unnecessary.

If you do something well, it's usually good enough. You don't have to make every thing you do perfect, because you'll get stuck in the trap of wasting time doing things that don't actually add value or make an impact.

I have a friend who used to work in an advertising agency in France. Her boss instilled this approach to her with the mantras: "Best is the enemy of good" and "Good is good enough."

You may want to start using these mantras in your own life. It could save you an enormous amount of time, energy, stress, and money.

IS GOOD REALLY GOOD ENOUGH?

It takes exponentially more work, time, and effort as you approach perfection while working on a task. That means, the longer you work to make something "just right," the longer you have to keep working to improve it just a little bit.

For example, if it takes you two hours to create a good presentation that will achieve your goals, it will probably take you twenty hours to create a near-perfect presentation. Sometimes, you may need to go all the way out to achieve a big goal, but most of the time a good presentation is good enough to get the job done.

The key is to know when you need to make something good enough, and when you need to go the extra mile to create something truly great. If you reflect on your life and you're honest with yourself, you'll realize that most of the time good is good enough. You may also reflect back on times when you really should have put in the extra work to create something truly great.

The problem with trying to do everything perfectly is that very few people will think all your extra work made any difference. Oftentimes, they won't even notice, and all that extra effort will have been in vain! This is the great tragedy of perfectionism.

Many good, smart, hard-working people waste countless hours trying to be perfect instead of being effective.

In other words, trying to make things 100% perfect is rarely worth the effort it takes to achieve it. And when it is worth it, you'll know you're working on something truly important and meaningful.

Perfectionism, in my opinion, is a crippling mental illness. That may sound a bit harsh, but having struggled with it for years myself, I've come to realize how devastating it is for artists and teachers. Perfectionism ruins our ability to share our gifts freely and locks us in a self-created cage of distorted fantasies that ensure we will never finish anything.

Nowadays I tell my clients a little anecdote to help them snap out of this trap.

Imagine you're on a boat with your best friends and the people you most love.

All of a sudden, someone who can't swim falls overboard and starts to drown.

You're the only one there who can save them. What will you do?

Will you do a few practice strokes in the pool? Will you go back to your cabin, do your hair, change into swim gear a few times and make sure you look perfect?

Or will you jump in, as you are, watch and all, and save them?

Think about this the next time you are stalling and chasing perfection like a heroin addict chasing the monkey. People need your help. Get in there and help them now.

If you give up perfectionism and aim for getting your projects and ideas done well, you can focus on the diamonds and achieve more in a month than you would in a year! And you'll have more time to relax and recharge.

When you're working on a task, figure out if good really is good enough, or if it's one of those few situations where you absolutely need to go the extra mile. Try it out and see what happens. You'll be pleasantly surprised at how much more you get done and how much more successful you'll become when you're focused on being effective instead of being perfect.

CHAPTER 5

ESSENTIAL MIND HACK #5

THE DELUSION OF TIME MANAGEMENT

One of the big reasons many people waste their lives running around and working hard while getting nowhere is the delusion of time management. The theory of time management has spawned an entire industry of people who believe that this thing called "time" is a limited resource, like gold, and needs to be managed. The propagators of this theory have created complex systems designed to help you slice your time up like a cake into neat little pieces where you cram in as many things as possible in the hope that if you can just put it in the calendar, you'll get everything done (and supposedly end up successful and happy).

This may sound pretty good in theory, but in practice, it's total BS and doesn't work. Those complex systems will never work for normal people for a few reasons:

1. ONLY ORDERLY PEOPLE CAN FOLLOW THEM

First, these time management systems are typically designed by and for pent-up military types who love the illusion of control and have a built-in drive to be organized and live by a rigid schedule. These types of people are already fastidious about their schedules to begin with; they eat, sleep, and crap at the same time every day. They don't need a time management system because they already live like a drill sergeant. It's how they're wired.

When it comes to living life, there are essentially two types of people. First are the "Organizers" who love to keep things organized and do well in more analytical jobs. The second are the "Creatives" who tend to be obsessed with creating stuff (and tend to be far less organized). Most of us are a combination of both, but one aspect will be more pronounced than the other.

Which are you? Are you an Organizer or a Creative? I'm guessing if you're reading this, you're a Creative. That's why you want to create something awesome in 21 days.

The Organizers will happily spend all day arranging their schedules into nice neat boxes, while the Creatives will have serious resistance to being locked into a schedule. And even if they do create one, they are likely to resent it and break it.

This is the first reason time management doesn't work. Creative types simply won't be able to use it. Go ahead and try. See if you can schedule your day to the minute and honestly stick to it with success. You'll probably end up neurotic and have a panic attack or rebel against it and go way off schedule on a mad, time-wasting binge of some kind.

Luckily, you don't need to worry about that. There is a much better way to get things done (and not live a regimented lifestyle). First you need to give up the illusion that you can "manage your time" at all.

2. THERE IS NO POINT IN BEING EFFICIENT AT LOW-VALUE WORK

The second, and possibly far more important reason time management fails miserably is facing up to the truth that 80% of what we do is highly ineffective. Even if we successfully manage to do everything on our to do list, 80% of it is pointless. Being highly efficient at wasting time is still a waste of time!

Think about it. If only a handful of things you do each day are actually highly valuable and lead you toward the things you want, then it's only by doing those few things that you will succeed in life. This is essential to realize.

We need to focus on the 20% of activities that matter most and abandon the rest. Abandon this notion of managing time and cramming your schedule full minute by minute. Instead, learn to focus on the most effective and useful 20% of things that really matter. If you accomplish your most important work each day, how could you possibly improve your productivity by working on something less important?

Do you want to be highly EFFECTIVE by doing the few things that matter most?

Or do you want to be highly EFFICIENT at doing things that don't matter at all?

I can create an awesome schedule for myself, with every single moment crammed with pointless low-value activities. I can do them all highly efficiently and be super productive and yet, at the end of the day, I've achieved NOTHING of value.

All I will have done is ticked off those boxes on the to do list I spent too much time creating, and in the process I will have deluded myself into thinking I've been successful because I followed my regimented program. Ticking boxes means nothing. Being efficient and productive doing low-value things means nothing. Having a day packed with stuff means nothing.

The only thing that matters is whether you are doing the FEW things that matter most. Do you know what they are, and are you doing them?

All the rest is the delusion of time management. We need to focus on the few things that matter, abandon the rest, and plunge head first into bringing our most important dreams to life.

3. TIME CANNOT BE MANAGED

Despite the many claims, no one has ever been able to "manage" time. Time isn't a thing you have to manage. Time isn't like a computer or system you can tweak and tune to your specifications. It's not like a chair you can have at your desk to sit on, or a relationship with someone that you can improve or end. Tomorrow doesn't really exist. Yesterday is just an idea, a memory. All you really have is now.

Right now. The eternal moment. This moment. You can imagine tomorrow, next week, or next year in your mind. You can plan to do countless wonderful things later on. But it's all imaginary. It's all in your head. It's all perception.

All you have right now is NOW. It's only when you are in the NOW that you can actually do anything. Can you do anything tomorrow or yesterday or next year? No. They don't exist until they become the now. Which is Now.

We only live life in the Now. Even thinking about the future can only happen in the Now. Nothing exists except the Now. Now is the moment of power. The power is Now.

Are you here? Are you aware you exist right Now? Whatever you want to do you can only do it Now. Right here. Right Now. This is it.

When you realize all you have is the Now, it becomes clear that time doesn't exist as an external thing you can manage because you don't get 24 hours. You just get now, now, now, now, now, now, now.

How long is now? How long is an hour (really)? Why do some days fly by and others drag on?

What is really going on?

All you ever have is the Now. And it's gone just as fast as it comes. You don't actually "have" any time at all.

So What Is Time?

Time is a concept we've invented to describe the movement of objects within space. Think about it. How do we measure time? It's based on movement. If everything in the universe were to stop moving tomorrow, the leaves stopped growing, the Earth and all the other planets froze in their exact positions, your body and all its systems stopped completely, every cell in your body stayed exactly as it was, all the atoms and subatomic particles in the universe stopped their movements, no thoughts occurred, if everything simply stopped moving and all changes ceased to occur at every level, what would happen to time?

It would stop. There would be no more hours or minutes. Just one long now. I don't want to get too far out here, but you need to get rid of the myth that managing time will solve your problems. The reason I'm bringing your attention to this is to help you get things done without all the neurosis of time management pie-slicing.

So since you can't manage time, what *can* you manage?

FORGET TIME MANAGEMENT; FOCUS ON SELF-MANAGEMENT

You can't manage time, but you *can* manage YOURSELF! This means managing your thoughts, words, actions, energy, and focus.

There are many things in life we can't directly change or control. We can't change the weather, other people, the size of the Earth, how atoms work, and a million other things. When we try to change things we can't control, we just end up disappointed, miserable, and depressed.

So we'd be wise to abandon "time management" and controlling things outside our sphere of influence, and instead focus all our energy on the things we can change.

This Means Mastering...

1. Your thoughts
2. Your emotions
3. Your words
4. Your actions

This is where you have power. This is where you have leverage.

You'll instantly feel more empowered when you make the great shift from trying to manage this abstract thing called time, and focus instead on the here and now, managing your own thoughts, feelings, energy, words, and actions.

Are you willing to stop trying to manage time and start managing yourself? We're talking about your moment to moment choices: the foods you eat, the thoughts you have, the words you use, and the influences you let in.

Focus on Managing Your Energy

Focus on making sure you invest your energy, your thoughts, words, and actions on the specific things that lead you to the greatest results. Make sure that in each MOMENT in the eternal now, **you are focused directly on achieving your goals.**

On a regular basis, stop what you are doing and ask yourself, "Is what I am doing right now moving me directly toward achieving my goals?"

If your answer is no, then you're wading about in the non-essential BS. It's time to clean it off and get back on point. If you start living in the Now and make sure what you're doing right now is directly connected to your mission, you'll never have to worry about time management again.

You can't manage time. You CAN manage your energy and how you use your energy to think, feel, and act. When you invest your energy in doing the things that create the results you want, you've used your "time" effectively. When you invest your energy in dragging a dead horse up a hill and dancing about in a pile of horse crap, you're not using your time effectively.

Are you serious about bringing your ideas to life? Then here is your challenge:

ASK YOURSELF THROUGHOUT THE DAY: "IS WHAT I AM DOING RIGHT NOW DIRECTLY MOVING ME TOWARD MY GOALS?"

If you want to really get things done, make sure everything you're doing is moving you directly toward your goals.

If not, change it. Stop what you are doing and do something better.

If you've truly made your most important work a priority, when you ask this question your answer will be YES at least 75% of the time.

Is what I am doing right now moving me directly toward achieving my goals?

The more you ask yourself this question, the more consciousness you bring to your daily life and the faster you'll start focusing on the top things that matter most.

Is what I am doing right now moving me directly toward achieving my goals?

There is just one last problem. In order for you to achieve anything, you need energy. It doesn't matter if you have a year free to do anything you want if you don't have the energy to do what you need to do. Nothing will happen, and you'll end up feeling like you're getting nowhere in life.

ENERGY MANAGEMENT AND CIRCADIAN RHYTHMS

Time management doesn't take into account your biology and your energy levels. If you've not slept well the night before, you're feeling totally wiped out, you have a headache, and you're barely able to drag yourself out of bed, how effective are you going to be during your 11:15 phone call? Or your 12:25 meeting with so and so, or your 2:47–3:15 writing session?

Time management is total nonsense because...

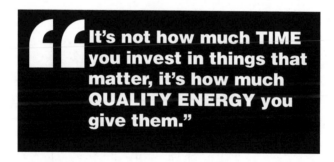

> It's not how much **TIME** you invest in things that matter, it's how much **QUALITY ENERGY** you give them."

If I'm writing and I'm super excited about it, PUMPED, and loving it, then what I write today is going to be effective, useful, and useable.

On the other hand, if I'm feeling spaced out, hungry, unable to think straight, and need a nap, guess what? I'll waffle my way through a couple hours of nonsense. Then, I'll have to go back and re-write it all later anyway.

Imagine you're having a meal with friends but you spend half the time fretting about something that's stressing you out and your focus and energy is away from your friends, and then you spend the other half of the time missing the conversation going on around you because you're texting someone who is not present about this worrisome problem. Were you really present with your friends?

Technically you were there, having a meal with your friends for two hours. You sat at the same table. You put in the time. Energetically though, you were not there—you were miles away. And guess what? Everyone noticed you weren't there. If you've ever had a conversation with someone who was checking their phone every two minutes, you know how that feels.

Likewise, you could be doing a job at an office for eight hours a day, but you're not really there for those eight hours. In fact, most office workers only manage to put in about two solid hours of productive work per day, and companies know this but still insist their employees sit there in their chairs pretending to be busy for the other six hours. Time management is a dangerous myth.

SO HOW DO WE GET THE BEST RESULTS AND REALLY GET THINGS DONE?

Like the ocean that has high and low tides, and the sun that sets and rises, your body too goes through natural cycles during which you're either "on"—you have more energy to do things—or you're "off," and you need to rest and replenish your energy.

This process is called the Circadian Rhythm and it affects all living things. **Humans have something called a biological circadian clock** that determines how our bodies naturally go through a pattern of low to high energy and back again each day. We don't have time to discuss this in detail here, but it's a fascinating subject well worth investigating. You can find out more about it by reading an awesome book called *The Power of Full Engagement* by Jim Lohr and Tony Schwartz.

Right now, I'm feeling the need to take a quick break. I could keep writing this section and contradict myself by going against the laws of nature and my own advice, or I could stop here and come back to tell you more when I'm fully refreshed. I'll tell you more in a moment.

Two hours have passed and I'm back. It's amazing what some food and a little rest can do! When our blood sugar levels drop too low, or we're simply overworked or fighting against our circadian clock, we can't function at our peak performance. It's like driving when the tank is almost empty and the engine begins to stammer and cut out. Just like your car, you won't perform well unless you've got enough gas in the tank.

Even if you know the top 20% actions to take, if you've got no energy, you'll end up lost in the 80% BS. You'll make mistakes and then need to go back and fix them later. Or you'll take far longer than usual to do what you need to do. Take a break and get back to it later.

It's essential that you organize your day to match your natural energy rhythms as much as possible and avoid forcing yourself to work in ways that go against your body and your own natural inspirations.

Let's figure out when you're going to be most focused by answering these questions:

What Time of Day Are You Naturally Most Inspired to Work: Morning, Afternoon, or Evening?

You will have far greater success in getting stuff done when you work during the time that you're naturally most alert, inspired, and at your best, rather than forcing yourself to work when you have less energy and focus.

For me, that means working in the morning, and the earlier the better. By about noon my energy levels have dropped and I'm not able to focus as well as I can in the morning. There is a time that works best for you—when is it?

When Are You Naturally Most Tired and Distracted?

It's important to know this so you can consciously allow yourself to rest and relax at those times and not stress yourself out by trying to work when you need to relax.

For me, I find that between 12:00 and 4:00 in the afternoon I'm least inspired to work. So rather than force myself to do things, I allow myself to rest, relax, sleep, read, or go to the beach. I know I'll just be wasting time if I try to do something important while I'm unfocused, so why not surrender to my natural rhythm and take good care of myself?

Life is not black and white, so having said all of the above you may find some days you are super inspired to work when you normally relax, and vice versa. If this is the case, then go with it. If you have a massive burst of energy to do something, go for it! Right now it's 12:50 p.m. when I'm normally not inspired to work, but I decided to keep writing anyway because I'm in the zone. When I get tired, I'll stop. But now I'm in the flow. I recommend you surrender to the flow as well.

Remember, the key is not how much TIME you put into something. It's about how much high-quality energy you invest.

Okay, now that you've broken free from the illusion of time management, you can start making amazing things happen in record speed. There is just one little problem....

CHAPTER 6

ESSENTIAL MIND HACK #6

THE RESISTANCE

"Resistance cannot be seen, touched, heard, or smelled. But it can be felt. We experience it as an energy field radiating from a work-in-potential. It's a repelling force. It's negative. Its aim is to shove us away, distract us, prevent us from doing our work."

— STEVEN PRESSFIELD

WHAT'S IN THE WAY IS THE WAY

As soon as you truly commit to a new way of living and doing, all hell breaks loose. Deal with it.

You can't do something new, significant, and meaningful without resistance from your ego scaring the life out of you. I wish you could, but once you're on your game, the impostors, the destructive parts of your psyche that were nicely settled in your life, suddenly take up arms and come to attack you with intent to kill. Once you start to get big things done, a revolt happens inside your mind and body that can take you down and destroy you. You're at war, and the Resistance is out to decapitate you.

How many times have you attempted to change and failed? Or your life got even worse? How many times were you doing great and then, from out of the blue, some crazy drama appeared that stopped you in your tracks?

This is all the work of the Resistance. The Resistance directly opposes your more noble intentions. It's your own personal rebel army in your head. If you don't learn how to deal with this aspect of yourself, change will simply be impossible.

Resistance is another name for your lower self, the lazy, addicted part of you. The part of you that simply wants to watch TV, eat junk food, have sex, and screw around doing nothing. Your lower self not only stops you when you are ready to change, but it also prevents you from being ready in the first place. That's why you've wasted so much time stalling and procrastinating. The Resistance fabricates circumstances to make change seem unattainable and the effort required not worth the hassle.

You know your inner Resistance has arrived when you find yourself avoiding the important things in life and feeling stuck.

SIGNS OF RESISTANCE:

1. Self-doubt
2. Being constantly distracted by meaningless entertainment
3. Wasting time on low-value work
4. Obsession with sex
5. Addictions (any kind)
6. Low energy, apathy, and depression
7. Starting new tasks or projects before you've finished old ones and rarely finishing anything you start

The Resistance has a 10,000-page book full of elaborate and convincing arguments. It's like an expert lawyer who can bend the truth and win any case.

"Why bother doing all that exercise when you don't know if it's ever going to work?"

"Can't you just get fit taking a magic pill?"

"You'll never lose weight anyway. You're a fat bastard and no one loves you."

"What's the point of taking the risk to set up that new business idea when most companies fail within three years?"

"Why bother taking risks when you can sit back and watch a movie and relax?"

"I'm too busy to start that new program to transform my life."

Your lower self, the Resistance within, distorts and hides information from your view. It misplaces important names in your head and deletes genius ideas from your memory.

For some, the Resistance is an emotion like fear or anxiety that consumes them, for others it's thoughts spinning in their mind, and for others the Resistance shows up as addictive behaviors. It doesn't matter so much how the Resistance shows itself to you. What matters is being aware of when it shows up to ruin your life and knowing how to overcome it. That's why this method is so important.

No matter how Resistance rears its ugly head in your life, one thing is certain: being trapped by our demons and limitations is no way to live. We're not here to pander to our lower desires and sacrifice our success. As long as we have no methods to deal with our lower self, we're going to stay stuck.

I hope by now you're getting a clear idea of what you're dealing with and what you're up against. If you've wondered why so few people change and why you've had such a hard time changing, there it is: the Resistance is lethal. It's heavily funded and knows exactly how to disarm, disappoint, and dismember you.

As long as you remain ignorant of how this force works and what it really is, you will never get anywhere in life. You will always fail. You'll live as a slave to your own mind while the Resistance sits on the throne and orders you to waste your precious life in distraction.

IT'S NOT ALL BAD...

The good news is that this Resistance is ultimately like a paper tiger or a dog whose bark is worse than his bite. Once you get to know Resistance and discover its lies, its illusions and trickery will start to lose power. Its genius is its manipulative nature and ability to seduce us, make us go unconscious, and "act out" compulsively as though we are in a hypnotic trance.

Once you "wake up" and get to know your Higher Self better, you'll begin to see the games being played out within you. Once you're aware what's going on, the real you can begin to claim your power back from this covert force within your own heart and mind.

If you want to be the master of your world and true creator of your life, this is your mission: to become highly conscious of who you are and know exactly what's really going on within you. Awaken the genius within and bust the Resistance when it appears.

Notice it. Call it out. See it for what it is...and get it done.

CHAPTER 7

ESSENTIAL MIND HACK #7

FEARS AND HALLUCINATIONS

> *"Fear keeps us focused on the past or worried about the future. If we can acknowledge our fear, we can realize that right now we are okay. Right now, today, we are still alive, and our bodies are working marvelously. Our eyes can still see the beautiful sky. Our ears can still hear the voices of our loved ones."*
>
> — THICH NHAT HANH

Behind the Resistance, procrastination, and sabotage in our lives there is often fear.

There are basically three kinds of fear.

1. Rational authentic fears
2. Unconscious irrational fears
3. Conscious irrational fears

RATIONAL AUTHENTIC FEARS

Fear isn't all bad. In fact, some fears are entirely healthy, supportive, and necessary for our success. We have rational authentic fear about the things we really should be afraid of. For example, if you are about to be hit by a bus, it's a damn good job that fear kicks in and gets you out of the way. If you're in a neighborhood that is known for burglaries and murder, it's wise to lock your door and be careful where you walk. If you're about to fall off a cliff, it's essential that fear alerts you to the danger and helps you pay attention. Fear of falling to your death could literally save your life. This kind of fear is invaluable and there is no need to change it, worry about it, or get rid of it. We need this kind of fear and we'd be wise to pay close attention to it.

However, the feeling of fear can often arise when it's not required and these other types of fear need to be addressed in a completely different way or we will become trapped in a false prison of our own making and live a shallow half-life of petty comforts and avoid our true calling.

UNCONSCIOUS IRRATIONAL FEARS

These kinds of fears are unconscious, so they don't make us sweat, stop breathing, start shaking, or freeze. This subtle, yet lethal, kind of fear subverts our success without our consciously knowing about it. This is our fear of unspeakable futures filled with imagined torment. It lurks beneath the surface of our awareness and stops us from moving forward without our realizing it. It does this by gently nudging us to avoid doing the things we need to do.

What are procrastination, perfectionism, distraction, and excuses? Fear in disguise. All these things are the *Resistance*.

Because fear often plays out below the surface of our consciousness, it may not be obvious it's even there, but like small doses of poison in our water, these unconscious fears infect us, weaken us, and sabotage our ability to show up fully and brightly for our lives. We don't realize they are sabotaging us, but as long as we keep allowing this toxic substance to poison our minds, we will never be able to take massive action and get it done.

The Most Common Fears

Many of these fears are unconscious, but they can still control you.

- Fear of the unknown
- Fear of failure
- Fear of success
- Fear of being overwhelmed and losing privacy if we get too famous
- Fear of being abandoned if we get too famous
- Fear of letting people down
- Fear of getting bad reviews or being hated
- Fear of getting sick
- Fear of being unloved
- Fear of not being good enough
- Fear of being a fraud
- Fear of not being able to keep it all going
- Fear of being uncomfortable
- Fear of slipping up

And ultimately...

- Fear of death

What are you afraid of?

What secret fears prevent you from taking action and doing what you need to do?

It's worth looking at this directly because if you don't face and expose your fears they will ruin your life. Your unconscious fears will sabotage you, and you won't even notice.

Once you identify and admit your fears, irrational as they may be, you can then spot them when they try to stop you. **Bringing consciousness to what is unconscious is the way we transform ourselves and stop repeating the past.**

What unconscious fears do you have?

Each of us has our own reason for playing small and sabotaging ourselves. At the core of it is usually some kind of fear of change. We don't like getting out of our comfort zone. Even though it's not really comfortable living in our comfort zone, at least we're used to it. It's a level of misery we can tolerate. Believe it when I say there's so much more to life than putting up with our self-imposed limitations and repeating the past.

CONSCIOUS IRRATIONAL FEARS

Simply by asking yourself a few questions, you can transform unconscious fears (that you can't do anything about) into conscious fears that you can face and overcome.

What are you afraid of?

How is unconscious fear ruling your life?

Look at the list of common fears and notice if any of those resonate with you.

I've noticed my own Resistance to make things happen is mainly *fear of success and fear of rejection*.

If I put this project out into the world, what happens next?

What if everyone loves me? What if I have to go on TV and talk to large groups of people? What if people reject me and I'm an outcast? What if no one likes me?

These things may seem trivial, but they are sabotaging our lives.

Why are you stopping yourself from being successful? What are you afraid will happen if you get everything you want?

Write it down....

Okay... did you write it down? Whatever you wrote down, there is a high likelihood that your fears will most likely not come true in real life. The reason it's important to write it down is so we can see how irrational our fears really are when they are reduced to words on paper in front of our eyes instead of allowed to run wild in our minds.

What are you afraid will happen if you're successful? Realize most of what we fear will never happen. Never. Fears exist inside our minds, in the framework of our perception. They do not exist in the world.

A bus coming toward you is real. You need to get the hell out of the way. Fear of everyone hating you because you publish a book is not real. Fear of dying because you do a product launch is not real. Fear that if you don't get something "perfect" you'll be persecuted is not real.

Most fears are simply not real. They are entirely in our heads, and only in our heads. My good friend Joshua BenAvides, author of *Break the Worry Habit,* writes, "Worry is the psychological habit of superimposing the imagination of future pain upon the present moment." He goes on to explain that worry and fear are entirely products of the imagination and have no bearing on what is real.

"Worry is a by-product of fear. And to live life with a constant, underlying fear of future pain is not to live at all. Fear and worry, more than anything else, are keeping people imprisoned and caged within the walls of their own imagination."

We look out into the world and project on it our irrational fears. The horrors we fear are hallucinations created in our minds. We're not actually afraid of the world. We're afraid of the illusory perceptions in our own mind.

- Are you willing to let go of these imagined fears?
- Are you willing to see your fears for what they are: illusions and hallucinations?
- Are you willing to accept that your irrational fears are nothing more than self-created hallucinations that exist solely in your mind?

MOVE PAST YOUR FEARS

Ralph Waldo Emerson said,

> *"Always do what you are afraid to do."*

Simply being willing to admit our fears are nothing more than imagination is profoundly liberating. Are you willing to move forward and have fun doing what you love? Just saying yes means you're already on your way to moving past your fears.

> *"The world we see that seems so insane is the result of a belief system that is not working. To perceive the world differently, we must be willing to change our belief system, let the past slip away, expand our sense of now, and dissolve the fear in our minds."*
>
> — WILLIAM JAMES

CHAPTER

8

ESSENTIAL MIND HACK #8

FOCUS

Most people fail to accomplish great things because they lack focus. The more ideas you have in your head, the more projects you'll be tempted to start. The more projects you start, the more scattered and fragmented your energy becomes and the less likely you are to complete any of them.

Have you seen those plate spinners who spin multiple plates on a pole? The more plates they spin, the harder it is to keep them all going. They run from one to the next desperately trying to keep them all moving, and the more plates they add, the harder it becomes until the plates either fly off and smash into a thousand pieces, or the plate spinner abandons the show and takes his bow. Either way, while it may feel fun in the moment, it's not sustainable and leads to either burn-out or being smashed to pieces. It's no way to live and it doesn't lead to results.

I know countless entrepreneurs (myself included) who have an impressive list of unfinished projects and an unimpressive list of completed projects. We do it because we see an idea in our mind as if it's already done, which is a wonder of the mind. The problem is that visualizing a finished project is not the same as bringing that idea into life. Not to mention, most things in life end up taking a lot longer than we ever imagined.

So if we really want to make some significant breakthroughs, we need to keep it simple and stay focused. We can still dream big, but we need to stop trying to make all our dreams come true at the same time and in the same way.

Being unfocused and spreading ourselves too thin is usually a symptom of a bigger problem. Often this endless spinning is simply covering up our irrational fears and avoiding the authentic suffering that comes with making things happen, creating an impact, and living an authentic life. It's a lot easier to be busy, busy, busy all day long than it is to stay focused and become successful and change the world. So the next time you notice yourself overwhelmed with too much going on, step back and look at what is really going on.

Why are you really doing this? What's really going on? What are you afraid of?

HOW TO STAY FOCUSED

To overcome this addiction to distraction remember the classic acronym— FOCUS.

Follow

One

Course

Until

Successful

This doesn't mean you have to only ever do one thing forever. It doesn't mean you're trapped with a ball and chain on your leg tying you to one idea for the rest of your life and you can't take a break or have variety in your life. What it does mean is that you are choosing to focus on one main project at a time and are bringing that one idea to completion *before attempting to complete another one.*

Focus on completing one project at a time.

If you are inspired to work a little bit on other projects while you finish one main project, it may be okay. But remember to invest the majority of your focus on ONE MAIN THING.

FOLLOW ONE COURSE UNTIL SUCCESSFUL

For the rest of this book, I highly encourage you to choose one main project you intend to complete and focus on that. Once you're successful with that project, you can use this same method to focus on another one, and another, and another, creating a long line of success stories.

Start now with ONE MAIN THING. What is the one main project you are going to focus on?

ESSENTIAL MIND HACK #9

HOW TO OVERCOME SELF-DOUBT

"Our deepest fear is not that we are inadequate. Our deepest fear is that we are powerful beyond measure. It is our Light, not our Darkness, that most frightens us. Joy is what happens to us when we allow ourselves to recognize how good things really are. Love is what we were born with. Fear is what we learned here. In every community, there is work to be done. In every nation, there are wounds to heal. In every heart, there is the power to do it."

— MARIANNE WILLIAMSON

Self-doubt can sabotage us before we even begin. The Resistance, the ego mind, tells us we're not good enough or we may fail so it's not worth trying. It tries to convince us to hold back, stay quiet, and look busy. It aims to keep us slaves locked inside an inescapable prison of complacency and sameness so we stay stuck and don't upset anyone by shining bright or being different.

The good news is we can sidestep the ego's games. Through compassion we can break free from self-doubt and worrying about how others may judge us.

Compassion arises when you open your heart to the pain of others and realize they need your help.

To create that liberating compassion, simply ask yourself the following question and consider the implications.

WILL YOU LET YOUR FRIEND DROWN?

Let's go back to that scene I painted earlier, the one I tell my clients who are holding themselves back from making things happen.

You're spending the day out on the ocean with your closest, dearest friends and one of them, the non-swimmer, falls overboard and begins to drown. Do you...

A. Go into your cabin to try on different swim gear to see what looks best for a rescue?

B. Go to the other side of the boat and practice your dive a few times so you get it perfect, and can impress everyone on board?

C. Jump in, right now, clothes, watch, and all and save your friend's life?

The answer is, of course, A. There is just no point in making a show of saving someone's life unless you're appropriately attired...

But seriously! This is what we're doing!

In our work, we stall, we worry about how we look, we tell ourselves false stories about how no one will like us unless we lose weight, or get a better camera, or design a new website, or whatever the excuse.

People are drowning!

They need your help. Now.

We think we're not ready and we need more practice.

Here's the truth: most people don't care how you look. They are dying on the inside. They are obsessed with bigger problems than yours and are hoping someone will reach out and rescue them.

Most people are far too distressed with their own problems to even give you a second of thought, but they will praise you forever if you jump in and help them.

Right now, literally billions of people need help. They're not hopeless cases. They just weren't taught how to swim. You can teach them. You can empower them. You can awaken them.

Have some compassion. Let your light shine.

Souls are calling out for support in so many different ways. Some of them are calling out to you, yes YOU personally. They need YOU. They need you to serve them and teach them how to swim.

Why me? You might ask.

Why not? You can swim better than they can. You can help. You can be of service.

You may not be the best swimmer the world has ever seen; you may not even have the most stylish swimsuit or a perfect bikini body. You may not have the world's most impressive dive, but you can swim. And countless people are drowning because they can't.

You don't need to be perfect. You just need to open your heart and let a little bit of that light shine.

Will you help them? Or are you too busy looking in the mirror?

Will you empower them?

You can reach out and change someone's life today, even in a small way.

You can open your heart and let yourself shine.

You can dive in.

CHAPTER 10

ESSENTIAL MIND HACK #10

DO IT NOW

The years are flying by. The world is changing so fast it's hard to keep up. Sooner or later this thing we call "life" will be over and we will leave these bodies and move on to the next place. Let's just stop for a moment and consider how precious our lives are and how fast moments of time are passing by.

Here we are in the eternal now...

This moment is here, now. And now it's gone. The last sentence you read is now only a memory in your mind, and as you read these words you are moving into the future one eternal moment at a time... one moment... after the next...

The Now.

Before you know it, a year will have passed. Then another. Then another and another. A decade will soon be gone. Each day our bodies get older and break down a little more. Each year is a year closer to our inevitable deaths.

Your body will soon die. And even if you're young and healthy, none of us can guarantee we'll be here tomorrow. Watch the news and you'll see plenty of young people dying from unexpected accidents.

In short, sooner or later you'll lose your chance to get your message out and share your gifts.

When you look back on your life, taking your last breaths, do you want to feel regret at how much you held yourself back? Or how much you shared your love and your gifts with others?

In the end, being "perfect" doesn't matter. What matters is did we enjoy being alive? Did we share our gifts and make a difference? Did we love and receive love?

Or did we waste our lives worrying about what people would think about us and trying to keep up with all the tedious things in life that ultimately don't matter?

In life, only a few things really have any impact. All the rest is essentially pointless. It's up to us to figure out what matters most and then plunge, head first, into those things with our complete heart and soul. Do it without a care in the world. Give freely, fully, completely.

Today could be our last day.

This could be our last month.

Let's make it matter.

Let's make it awesome.

Let's have some fun!

ESSENTIAL MIND HACK #11

DO LESS WORK TO GET MORE DONE

I'd love to think it's possible to go work on our mission all day every day, every week, every year, and never rest. The reality is that we genuinely require time off to replenish our energy and re-ignite our inspiration. We also need to enjoy simply being alive and not having our entire world be dominated by producing stuff. Life is more than just work. Your self-worth is not tied to your productivity, although many people think it is. The unconscious belief that drives most people to overwork can be summarized as follows.

You have no innate value. Your value is entirely derived from producing something valuable, or at least looking busy. If you are busy, you are important. If you take time off, you are a slacker and should be ashamed of yourself. Get back to work!

The problem with this belief is if we work, work, work, we will eventually crash and burn. This might mean getting sick, depressed, or having an accident. It could also mean we ignore the most important people in our lives, destroy our relationships, and end up lonely and heartbroken.

We didn't come to this planet just to work our asses off all day every day. We're also here to enjoy life, relationships, beauty, adventure, travel, and fun!

It's harder for some people than it is for others to stop and relax, but no matter who we are, we all need time out to enjoy the richness of life.

Let's first get clear about why this is so important and then I'll share with you some powerful, easy methods to take rewarding breaks and come back feeling awesome.

WHY YOU NEED BREAKS

If we don't have enough physical energy, we simply won't be able to do anything. If we feel exhausted or suffer from blood sugar crashes, sleep deprivation, adrenal fatigue, dehydration, or any number of health challenges, we can't do quality work. High value creativity requires energy, vibrancy, and a clear, sharp mind. Sickness, crankiness, fatigue, and lethargy are not conducive to inspiration.

Breaks also allow us to gain a different perspective on our work. How many times have you had a great idea in the shower or while out doing something non-work related? Or been stumped by a problem at work for hours only to let it go, sleep on it, and wake up knowing the solution? Almost all creative people will tell you that taking time away from work allows them to see the work from a new perspective and come up with creative ideas and solutions that were not obvious while they were working for 12 hours straight.

Painters and photographers repeatedly physically step back from their compositions to see them from a new perspective. Authors regularly take walks between writing sessions to allow creative ideas to flow. No matter what you're doing, you need these changes in perspective in order for your work to be the best it can be.

Finally, if your entire life revolves around your work, you can miss out on the other blessings that make being alive wonderful and truly enjoyable.

Being human is a complex and miraculous experience. Having meaningful relationships with people we love, spending time enjoying nature, art, food, and trying out new activities, traveling to new places, going on spiritual retreats, all these things and more can have a profoundly positive impact on our lives and nourish us on a deeper level.

Without these other aspects of being human, our lives can become lopsided and eventually lead us to regretting our choices. On their death beds, many people have serious regrets about having spent too much time working and not enough time enjoying life and being loving toward others. It's better to learn this lesson now than to wait until it's too late.

Having said that, creative people on a mission tend to be more obsessed with their work and live less balanced lives than those who are not on a mission. This means that in order for you to give your all to make an impact, you'll end up spending more time doing the work than someone who's not on a mission. If what you're doing is truly your life's work and it's deeply meaningful to you, you'll feel nourished by your work and it will call to you. Even so, it's still important to take breaks and make sure you're healthy and happy.

The bottom line is that no matter how passionate you are, your body and mind need rest and rejuvenation to be able to drive at your highest potential. If you neglect this, your work and your life will suffer.

To be highly productive we also need to be great at taking breaks.

WHAT'S THE MOST EFFECTIVE WAY TO TAKE BREAKS?

1. Take a solid break for at least two hours every day.

2. Take a whole day off every week.

3. After you've completed your project, congratulate yourself and take a few days off to create a distinct end to one project and get ready for your next one.

LET'S DO IT!

Now you know the essential insights to get it done, so let's get on with it. As you read this, keep in mind the faster you APPLY everything you learn, the better. Don't waste time trying to understand everything perfectly. Focus on ACTION. Learn and apply. Learn and apply. Let's go!

PART II

THE UNSTOPPABLE 21 DAY CHALLENGE

Going to **WAR** with the Resistance and Becoming Unstoppable

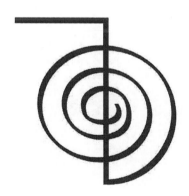

"The only impossible journey is the one you never begin."

— ANTHONY ROBBINS

CHAPTER 12

WAR: THE SECRET FORMULA

MAKE THE IMPOSSIBLE POSSIBLE AND BECOME UNSTOPPABLE

"Resistance's goal is not to wound or disable. Resistance aims to kill. Its target is the epicenter of our being: our genius, our soul, the unique and priceless gift we were put on earth to give and that no one else has but us. Resistance means business. When we fight it, we are in a war to the death."

— STEVEN PRESSFIELD, *THE WAR OF ART*

After seven years of research and personal experimentation, I finally discovered and refined a method to give procrastination and Resistance such a good whack around the head that it knocks it unconscious. Most people have wonderful ideas and dreams but their inner Resistance sabotages them from bringing their precious dreams to life.

In the 18th chapter of the Mahabharata Epic, known as the Bhagavad Gita, a story is told of a man named Arjuna who finds himself on a battlefield with no idea how to win the war. With the help of a Higher Power, he learns that the real war is the one inside of him, and that this is a battle with his inner demons.

The Bhagavad Gita says,

> *"The impermanent has no reality; reality lies in the eternal. Those who have seen the boundary between these two have attained the end of all knowledge. Realize that which pervades the universe and is indestructible; no power can affect this unchanging, imperishable reality. The body is mortal, but that which dwells in the body is immortal and immeasurable. Therefore, Arjuna, fight in this battle."*

This story relates to our own lives and the inner war we face. If we allow the enemy to defeat us, it will. Yet if we take a stand for the sacredness of our own lives and purpose, and arm ourselves with an unstoppable method to win, we become destined for victory.

TURN YOUR LIFE INTO A SERIES OF SUCCESSFUL ADVENTURES

As you embark on this journey, you will realize you truly are the hero of your own life. The hero chooses to take a risk, ventures into the unknown, faces their demons and challenges, and comes back with the elixir that will make the world a better place. Ideas are just the start. The real challenge is making things happen and then doing it again and again.

This is your chance to make the heroic journey from ideas, theories, and inspirations to real word results. This is how you create something new by mastering the nitty-gritty details of bringing a meaningful project to life. You're about to learn a repeatable process that you can use to achieve any project, idea, or dream.

The aim of this 21 day challenge is to turn each month into a fun, exciting, revitalizing journey. Each month is a new opportunity for success. Each month you do the things that matter most for you. AND you enjoy quality time off to relax, renew, and enjoy!

The following Unstoppable 21 Day Challenge allows you to win the war against your inner demons and outer challenges. It shows you exactly how to bring your ideas into reality and enjoy an extraordinary life step-by-step.

By using this proven method, you will have the power to achieve things in your life you'd never imagined possible. Apply it fully and you'll be amazed at what you can create.

There are three stages to the Unstoppable 21 Day Challenge:

WHACK!

ACT.

RELAX.

Or WAR for short.

Because you are at war with your own Resistance, you are held back by all the limiting beliefs, self-sabotage, and little excuses. This stops you from becoming who you were born to be. What stands between you and your success is the Resistance. The three stages of WAR allow you to drop a bomb once and for all on all the self-imposed limitations and excuses that have held you back.

By embarking on this journey, you become a master of your destiny, an incognito warrior. You claim back your power and create a life of adventure.

THE UNSTOPPABLE 21 DAY CHALLENGE— A QUICK OVERVIEW

STAGE 1:

W = WHACK! The pre-challenge set up—winning before you start

Get clear on your 21 day challenge game plan and win the battle before it's ever fought.

STAGE 2:

A = ACT! Get it done! Doing the Unstoppable 21 Day Challenge

Take massive action for 21 days and make the impossible possible.

STAGE 3:

R = RELAX! Celebrate and Renew

Your post-challenge break to rest, rejuvenate, celebrate, and prepare for your next mission.

These three stages combined give you the power to wage WAR with Resistance— and win. Time and time again.

WHACK. ACT. RELAX.

PREPARE. WORK. CELEBRATE.

CLARIFY. CREATE. REJUVENATE.

These three stages of making things happen make you unstoppable.

Let's take a closer look at how it works.

STAGE 1: W = WHACK! THE PRE-CHALLENGE SET UP—WINNING BEFORE YOU START

"Every battle is won before it's ever fought."

— SUN TZU

WHACK is at the core of the Unstoppable 21 Day Challenge because by doing this first stage right, you severely disable the Resistance before you start. This means the war inside you is already won before you even begin on day one of your 21 day challenge.

World-class athletes and military leaders alike know every battle is first won in the mind. If your mindset and preparation are lacking, success is impossible. Lack of foresight and poor preparation sink countless dreams before they even see the light of day. This inner war is real, and it is sapping the joy out of billions of people every single day.

Most people fail to achieve their goals and aspirations, not because they are lazy (although some are), but because they stumble toward them like lambs to the slaughter, utterly unprepared, with no clear plan or action and hopelessly underestimating the enemy.

The enemy, the Resistance, is omnipresent and lives within everyone like a virus. It strikes us most when we're weak. It holds us back from our own greatness. It's on a relentless mission, scheming up elaborate ways to distract and dishearten us as we fumble through life searching for success but never quite getting there.

If you want to be successful and happy, you must recognize the enemy clearly and win the WAR for your mind and your life. Ignorance is not bliss; it's suicide. If we don't realize what we're up against, we'll end up throwing away our lives to a merciless saboteur, and we will fail to achieve our mission in life.

The 21 Day Challenge WHACK system is critical because without foresight and methods to achieve success, we will remain trapped in the spiral of overwhelm, distraction, sabotage, and despair.

The good news is that armed with the WHACK system, you'll destroy obstacles and Resistance before you begin.

I call it WHACK because this system works like a weapon against the seductive lies of procrastination, laziness, and living an inauthentic life of toxic, shallow pleasures.

> **" WHACK is important because most of us have a pretty good idea about what we want and what we need to do—but we're not doing it!"**

Lack of knowledge isn't the problem. Lack of action is. WHACK takes care of that.

By applying the WHACK system to your life, you'll never be the same—and I mean that. WHACK is such a powerful weapon that it annihilates procrastination from your life and turns you into an unstoppable results creator. Once you start using your WHACKing stick, you will become almost superhuman. You'll be able to achieve up to 16 times more results than you were getting before in the same amount of time. It's like you now have access to superpowers that have been locked inside you. Now the dreams and goals you most cherish are manageable, even fun, and every day, every week, and every month becomes an opportunity for a personal breakthrough.

Here's a quick introduction to the WHACK system.

WHACK—THE SECRET WEAPON TO WIN BEFORE YOU BEGIN

W = What Do You Want?

Define your goal. Get clear on the what, why, when, and where of your idea.

H = How Will You Make It Happen?

Craft a simple plan that moves your projects forward in the fastest, easiest way possible. You don't need to know everything, just the first steps.

A = Absolute Accountability

Set up solid accountability to do what you need to do so your success becomes inevitable. With absolute accountability, you're no longer left alone with your excuses to fester and distract you. This means getting an outside source of accountability and setting up consequences for NOT showing up and doing your work. These consequences get your ego on board and allow you to do things with remarkable ease that you've been putting off.

C = Conditions and Structures

What are the situations you need to set up in your life to make it EASY for you to succeed? In this step, we create the ideal conditions and structures for you to take massive action so it's impossible for you to fail.

K = Kick-Start

With kick-start, you'll create a weekly and daily action plan so you know what your most important work is every single day.

So there it is: WHACK! The secret weapon to win before you begin. Failure is no longer in the cards. You'll become someone who takes massive action and gets things done. Success will be yours.

Once you've completed this stage, you'll know exactly what you want, how to do it, and have knocked Resistance unconscious. You'll be living in a new reality. As if by magic, you'll find that you can make things happen like never before, and you'll be excited to dive into your 21 day challenge with confidence and power.

Then, it's time to act!

STAGE 2: A = ACT! GET IT DONE! DOING THE UNSTOPPABLE 21 DAY CHALLENGE

Get on your hero's journey, take massive action for 21 days, and make the impossible possible.

> *"It is one thing to study war and another to live the warrior's life."*
>
> — TELAMON OF ARCADIA

By Stage Two, you know exactly what you want to achieve and how to make it happen in record speed. Now is the time to embark on your 21 day challenge, get it done, and fulfill your mission.

So far you've simply been preparing yourself for the journey. The 21 day challenge is where the rubber meets the road. It's where you, the hero of your own life, have accepted the call to adventure and are now on your mission to bring your ideas to life. This is where you travel from where you are now into your vision of where you want to be.

Each day, over a 21 day period, you'll wake up inspired to taking highly effective actions that lead you directly toward your destination. During this period, you'll find yourself doing remarkable things you never imagined possible and creating outstanding results.

This is where your strength and resolve will be tested. The Hero's Journey is about deep transformation on all levels. It's about you, the hero in your own life, fulfilling your purpose, taking action and making your projects, goals, dreams, and desires actually manifest in physical form. It's about the remarkable act of creating something new that has never existed before and changing the world. It's about taking risks and being willing to fail. It's about taking the chance to experience magic and bliss, and to return with the treasures of experience, happiness, success, money, and the joy of knowing your life is embedded with meaning.

The Hero's Journey is about letting go of who you were yesterday and discovering who you really are and what you're really capable of achieving now—today.

Your life is a remarkably complex and magical story. You came here into this world for a reason. And it's your divine duty to discover that reason and then act upon it.

On day 21, you will have achieved your goals, and you'll be ready for a well-earned break, which leads us to the final stage of the 21 day challenge.

STAGE 3: R = RELAX! CELEBRATE AND RENEW

Now that success has been achieved, it's time to celebrate your victories and enjoy yourself! Stage three is your post-challenge break to rest, rejuvenate, celebrate, and prepare for your next mission. Here you take the time away from the work to enjoy yourself, celebrate your victory, and bask in your success. It's time to let go of work and enjoy playing. You deserve it! You are a hero.

In this final stage of the Unstoppable 21 Day Challenge, you can do fun things you've been putting off for too long and really enjoy yourself and your life. Some people go on that vacation they've been dreaming about, others unplug the internet and enjoy just being at home, reading, relaxing, and taking care of things. Others throw an extended party or set off to the wilderness to be fully unplugged and away from it all. The possibilities are endless.

Whatever you want to do to celebrate is up to you. It's your life, and you can take the opportunity to embrace it fully and deeply. Many people who do take this time to relax and celebrate find that just taking time off to have fun is by itself a huge success and big dream achieved after years of overwork.

Most of us are so used to working ourselves to death without a break that taking time off to congratulate ourselves and enjoy life is a massive success on its own.

This means, simply by choosing to take this time off to relax and enjoy, you may feel like you're going from one successful mission—achieving great things—to another successful mission—enjoying your time away, venturing off, and enjoying yourself in new ways filled with a sense of wonderful achievement.

IMPORTANT NOTE: To get the most from your celebration, make sure you set it up and plan for it right at the beginning of the 21 day challenge before you even start working on your project. Don't leave it to the last minute. Do it at the beginning.

The Unstoppable 21 Day Challenge is designed to be fun and bring back the joy and excitement into your life. It's a way to play a bigger game on your own terms and do things you've always dreamed about. It's about making your whole life meaningful, magical, and powerful.

SUCCESS UPON SUCCESS UPON SUCCESS

After you've gone through this complete process once, you'll be able to use these same methods to make other things happen in your life with lightning speed. You can use this for anything from getting a project finished in 21 days to quitting an old habit or creating a new one, losing weight, getting physically strong, and almost anything else you want to do.

This method is literally life changing because it forces you to do your best work and give up all the excuses that have held you back in the past. Instead of getting up each day and muddling through life, half hoping your dreams will somehow happen, you now have the power to focus your attention and effort on the few things that matter most.

This method allows you to go from passive to active. It focuses your energy on the most effective actions to bring your biggest goals and best work into life. It transforms you into a pro who gets things done and who walks the talk. It gives you the key to the super powers that were locked inside you.

IT GETS EASIER AS YOU GO

This method may appear a little complex the first time you do it, like learning to drive a car. But once you get the hang of it, you can jump in, turn the keys, and get going on your adventure effortlessly.

I highly recommend you read through this whole process before you start your 21 day challenge.

The first time you apply the Unstoppable 21 Day Challenge method it will take longer—after that it gets easier and easier because you'll see your success expanding and your adventures becoming more fun and rewarding. I can now set up a 21 day challenge in under 30 minutes, and you'll be able to do the same.

And to make this entire process profoundly easier for you, I've also included The Unstoppable Master's Program—which includes exclusive bonus videos and audios to show you exactly how the whole process works and gives you shortcuts and bonus tips so each time you embark on your 21 day mission, it's more fun, more powerful, and more enjoyable. Make sure you access your Unstoppable Master's Program because it will help you implement the methods you're learning easier and faster.

You can access this free bonus program at:

awakenedacademy.com/21daybonus

THE UNSTOPPABLE
21 DAY CHALLENGE

3 STAGES

W A R

WHACK. ACT. RELAX!

THE UNSTOPPABLE
21 DAY CHALLENGE

STAGE 1

WHACK

THE SECRET WEAPON TO
WIN BEFORE YOU BEGIN

CHAPTER 13 | WHACK: THE W'S— WHAT DO YOU WANT?

WHAT, WHY, WHEN, AND WHERE

We activate your whacking powers with clarity. What do you want to achieve? What is the end result you want? It may seem obvious, but unless you know exactly what you want to do, you can't do it. Lack of clarity about the end result or final destination is one of the biggest driving forces of procrastination. If we don't know where we're going, we can't plan to get there.

How do we know how close we are, or when we've arrived?

Vagueness and drifting leaves us settling for less and living unfulfilling lives that just sort of happen. Vagueness allows us to drift from one crisis to another without ever finishing anything or making significant steps forward. After all, how can we go forward when we don't know where we're going?

If you don't have an idea of what you want or where you want to end up, you'll invariably end up at the whims of other people's desires, floating around like driftwood in the ocean, tossed and turned by the waves and tides of life. If you're exceptionally lucky, you might end up on a beautiful beach somewhere, but if you leave your life to others, you're far more likely to find yourself washed up in some toxic swamp and wondering how the hell you got there. Don't let that happen. Even if you've found yourself washed up in a life you despise, today can be different. Today you can escape. Today you can choose your course and start moving forward. You can take the time right now to get clear on what you want and call in all your energy to serve your highest impact work.

WHAT DO YOU WANT TO MANIFEST IN THE NEXT 21 DAYS?

In this first stage, you'll get super clear about:

- What you want to achieve (the end result of your work or project)
- Why it's important to you (what's your deeper motivation?)
- When you want to get it done (the deadline)
- Where and at what time of day you will do it (physical location and time dedicated to your success)

Getting this clarity will deliver the first blow to that annoying inner voice that's been sabotaging your life and holding you back. Life is simply too short to waste on trivial things. Each second counts, so sift through the trivial and find the diamond. Consider this question to help you get oriented toward what's REALLY important:

IF YOU ONLY HAD 21 DAYS LEFT TO LIVE, WHAT WOULD YOU DO?

There may be a lot of things you would like to do, so let's to do a brain dump for starters. A brain dump gets all those ideas, worries, and thoughts out of your head and heart and onto paper. Writing things down is extremely powerful. It's the first step to overcoming the beast of procrastination and turning the mess of the mind into clarity on paper. Just getting your pen and paper now gives those inner voices that have been running your life their first WHACK! It also gives you the power to make progress.

Investing time to do this will be paid back to you countless times over. So grab a pen and paper (or a computer) and answer the following questions:

Step 1: What Do You Want to Do?

Write down *all* the things that are unfinished and stressing you out. Write down everything you'd love to achieve in the next 21 days. Just get them all out of your head and onto paper. Do this now and don't hold back. It will feel deeply relieving.

Step 2: Pick ONE THING to Work on for the Next 21 Days

There may be a long list of unfinished tasks and ideas you have written down, and you may feel the urge to do them all. In time, you may be able to take them all on. But for now, just pick ONE to focus on achieving in the next 21 days. Make sure it's something extremely valuable to you and possible to achieve in 21 days. Keep asking yourself the question, "If you only had 21 days left on this planet, what would you do?" This question helps focus the mind.

For your success, it's essential you choose something that you believe is possible to achieve in 21 days. The mind can imagine all kinds of finished projects and make it seem as if it's going to be easy and simple. So taking this into consideration, make sure to strike a reasonable balance.

You know yourself and your schedule better than anyone, so be honest and push yourself as far as you can without making yourself snap. If you pick something that's doable, you'll gain momentum and feel even more confident that you can do more. If anything, make the first attempt at this something fairly easy and then increase the challenge for your next 21 day challenge. Remember, the aim here is to do this over and over again, so each month is fun, exciting and successful.

How should you decide which project to work on first? Chances are you know in your gut what the most important thing to do is. It's probably winking at you now. Look at your list and pick the one thing that you need to do more than anything else. If it's not possible to complete anything on your list in 21 days, then just chunk down your ideas into smaller bits and pick one piece for your 21 day challenge. For example, if you're writing a thousand-page book, don't try to write the whole thing in three weeks. Just pick a number of chapters you're inspired to write, or a number of words you commit to writing and have that as your challenge.

If you're still not sure, look at all your potential ideas and ask yourself:

What's the top 20% idea that will create the biggest positive impact in the least amount of time?

Is it something that's going to lead to a tangible result?

Make sure you're doing something meaningful and that you're confident you can achieve in 21 days. If you're still not clear, recognize your uncertainty as just another form of procrastination and simply pick the easiest one to do!

Sometimes in life we have a 49/51 situation where two options are almost equally good. If that's the case, close your eyes and just pick one so you can move forward. The main thing is to choose and move on so you don't stay stuck. Let's do it.

WHY IS THIS IMPORTANT TO YOU?

Now that you know what you want, let's make sure you have the energy to get it done. One of the most powerful forces behind getting it done is having a clear grasp of WHY you want to do it.

Your BIG WHY is the deeper reason you do what you do. Behind your actions, unseen forces motivate you to either do or not do things. It's time to find out what makes you so excited to get it done.

Exercise: Finding Your "Why" and Your "Why Not"

Imagine you've already finished the project you've picked. You're now already successful. It is done, you're awesome, and you're successful. Close your eyes and clearly see and feel what it's like to have completed your mission.

Once you see it for a while, answer these questions:

- Why is your life better now that you've done this thing?
- How do you feel?
- Why is this important for you?
- What other benefits do you notice now that it's done?

Once you've written down all the positive things you'll experience by finishing your mission, let's now get clear on the negative things you are going to avoid by doing it. Why is this so important? We are often motivated to avoid pain. Use this tendency to your advantage and get super clear about how your life will suck if you don't do it.

Take a few moments to list all the unpleasant things that can happen if you DON'T do it.

Write it down so you feel the pain of procrastination. Write it all down so you really feel the excitement of doing it and the pain of not doing it.

- What will happen if you DON'T do it?
- How will your life be WORSE if you don't do it?
- Who will you let down if you don't do it?
- What negative things will you feel if you don't do it?
- What are all the negative consequences of procrastinating on this?

Once you've written this down, you'll have your WHY. You'll know you're clear when you're excited about it. If you feel some anxiety, fear, or worry about it, that's fine. In fact, the more emotional you are the better because it shows you're really serious. If you're not feeling excited or at least a little anxious, go back and pick something else. Why waste time on random nonsense that leads nowhere and makes you feel like you're wasting your life?

SET YOUR DEADLINE

Now that you know what you're going to do and why it's important to you, let's get a completion date down. Without a date it's just a bunch of hopeful fantasies and wishful thinking that's never going to happen. Dates create focus. Dates help us prioritize. Dates make sure we stop screwing around and start bringing our ideas and dreams to life.

WHAT'S YOUR DATE?

When is the deadline for this thing you've picked? Pick a specific day.

Write it down clearly. Give yourself enough time, but don't put it off too far or it will not have any power.

I will finish _____

_____ by _____.

Awesome! Doesn't it feel good to have this level of focus and clarity?

WHERE WILL YOU PHYSICALLY BE WHEN YOU DO THIS?

Will you be at home at your desk? Will you need to go somewhere? Will you be in the car, on a bus, in a plane, in an office, or in the wilderness?

Get a clear image of yourself in this place doing whatever it is that you need to do. Visualize yourself completing the task at hand. Write down where you will be.

TIE IT ALL TOGETHER

Complete this statement so your intention is super clear to you:

I commit to_____

_____

by_____.

This is important to me because _____

_____

I will work on this _____ every _____ to get it done.

For example, here is what I created for this project:

I commit to finishing the 21 Day Challenge book and having the website ready *by* Sept 1st 2018.

This is important to me because it will allow many souls to move forward with more power and will also help me make things happen every month, increase my income, impact lives, and illuminate the path of action.

I will work on this at my desk *every* morning until lunch *to get it done.*

This level of clarity is powerful. We must also ground the intention and make it real by adding some simple images, words, or objects to a space that will remind you of your mission.

VISION BOARD

It's helpful to have a vision board of your success so that every day you can see where you are going and feel inspired by it. You can radically improve your ability to take action by creating an image or collection of images of the FINAL RESULT of your work. By putting your vision board somewhere you can see it every day, you're rewiring the neurons in your brain and reminding yourself to focus on turning your vision into a reality.

For example, if you are writing a book, create a mock up-cover (or pay someone $5 on Fiverr.com to do one for you), print it out, and wrap it around a book, or just print it out and stick it on the wall.

The more you can clearly see where you're going, the easier it is to stay motivated and keep taking action.

Consistently Remind Yourself of the End Result

Your vision board can include images of finished products, pictures of you feeling great, images of happy customers, or successful people who have benefited from your work. Get creative. Any image that represents to you the final success of your project will work great.

The key is to make sure you *feel good* when you see it. If it inspires you, it's great. If not, change it until you feel inspired. You can use symbols, images of nature, color, or anything else that helps you experience the end result of your success. Take a few minutes to think about and imagine what that would be like.

Once you have some ideas, go ahead and print them out, get them created, or in some way bring them to life. As soon as you do this, you'll instantly feel as if you're doing this for real and you'll notice a shift in your energy around your project.

Where to Put Your Vision Board

In feng shui, different areas of the home are associated with different activities or aspects of life. If you already know about feng shui, then I suggest you put your visions in the career area of your home. If you're not aware of feng shui, don't worry, just put your images somewhere that you see them often. For example, on a wall facing your desk where you work or somewhere you'll notice it repeatedly throughout the day while you're creating your project.

Taking the time to design a custom image for your vision board may take a while to accomplish. You can just put ONE object or one image somewhere to inspire you. This can be as simple as placing an inspiring book on your desk or printing out an image of happy people and sticking it to a wall you see frequently throughout the day. Every time you see your image or object it will remind you of your goal. As an example, I have printed out the words "21 Day Challenge" and posted it in front of my desk to remind me of this project and make sure I finish it! Now, go find one inspiring object or image that reminds you of your success and place it somewhere you'll see it often. Do it now and you'll feel better right away.

WH**A**CK:
THE H—
THE HOW

HOW ARE YOU GOING TO MAKE THIS HAPPEN?

Knowing what you want is only part of the equation. Many people have great vision and fabulous ideas, but when you ask them how they intend to make it happen they go silent, shuffle about sheepishly, and stare at their feet in embarrassment.

Vision without action is hallucination. Action without vision is neurosis.

To actually bring this idea to life in 21 days, we need a clear vision AND a solid plan that enables us to move closer and closer to our visions and goals, one step at a time.

Your vision is your destination. Your plan is the route you are going to take to reach your destination. Just as physically traveling from one place to another tends to have many routes and modes of transportation, so does your goal. You can take a car, bus, train, plane, helicopter, or walk, but not all routes and methods of transport are created equal. No two roads to a destination give you the same experience, but they can bring you to the same place. Some routes are more enjoyable, easy, and fun while others are harder and take more time. Some routes are doomed to failure. Be careful, some paths will deceive you and lead you astray, washing you up somewhere, depleted and far from where you are meant to be.

If you figure out the best route for you to achieve your goals before you begin, you can save yourself time and stress. If you don't, you may end up wasting a lot of time and achieving very little. Take time to create a route to your destination that makes the most sense and is most effective for you.

NOT ALL PATHS ARE EQUAL

Some things you do move you rapidly toward the goals you want. While other things you do may appear to be helpful, but they don't really help you reach your goals. For example, if your goal was to create an awesome meal for friends, you could make a dish you've never tried before, waste a day screwing it up in the kitchen, get stressed, waste money, and end up with a charred mess that ruins the evening for everyone. Or, you could make something you've made before and know your guests will love and will only take you an hour to prepare. What's a better use of your time? What is your plan to make it happen? How are you going to bring your ideas to life?

As you do this process, remember that the map is not the same as the territory, and all plans are subject to change. This means that you can relax a little, be open to ideas, and just do the best you can knowing full well that your plans could and probably will change once you get started.

EXERCISE: FIGURE OUT THE BEST ROUTE TO YOUR DESTINATION

Step 1: Where Do You Want to Go?

Write down what you want to achieve. What is your vision or destination? If you did the last exercise you will already know this. If you don't know, go back and get clear on this first!

Step 2: Create Your Plan

Write down the best plan you can think of to achieve that result. What steps need to happen for you to go from A to B? How will you go from where you are now to where you want to be?

For example, if you're on a mission to finish your book in 21 days, your plan may look like this.

- Get clear on Title
- Write first draft
- Take time to get away from book and spend time in nature
- Write second draft and upgrade
- Write third draft
- Write fourth draft
- Send to a few trusted readers to get feedback
- Add feedback
- Send to editor
- Finalize

Step 3: Put Things in Order

Your plan is your route to get you from where you are now to where you want to be. GPS apps like Google Maps and others allow you to plug in your destination (your vision). Then they show you a map with step-by-step directions to get from your starting point to your destination. If the directions were not in order but randomized, what would happen? Instead of telling you what road to take next, it may tell you what road to take 15 steps from now. You can't take that turn until you physically reach that part of your journey. If you tried to follow GPS directions out of sequence you'd probably get extremely frustrated and end up lost pretty quickly.

When it comes to making things happen, the same thing is true. You need to organize your next steps sequentially so you can keep moving forward one step at a time. To do this, look at your list of things that need to happen and re-order them so you can follow your plan step-by-step.

Step 4: Upgrade Your Plan

Now, here's where it gets interesting. Look at your plan and ask yourself:

- How could I do LESS work or take less time and get the same result?
- How could my plan be at least four times faster and four times easier?

If you can get help in an area you're not good at, it can save you countless hours. Sometimes certain steps can be combined or removed completely. There's almost always an upgraded choice if you're willing to think differently and be open to new possibilities outside the box.

For example, let's imagine you need to fix a problem with your website but you're not a web developer. You could spend weeks figuring out HTML and javascript to solve the problem, or you could just talk to someone who already knows exactly how to solve the problem and get it fixed today.

What's going to get you the results you want? In many cases, we can get trapped and lost in over-analyzing and trying to figure things out on our own. We can end up spending months and months going in circles until we finally give up! That's not effective.

Relax. Allow your genius mind to give you a better plan that will save you time and energy. There is always a more effective, easier way to do things. What is it?

Write it down. See what comes up now....

How could you be more effective, do less, and achieve more?

This step is magical.

Don't just skip it if you're not getting instant answers. Keep asking the question, "How could I do less and achieve an even better result?" Allow your genius mind to give you the answers. The best answers will most likely come to you when you're relaxed, so keep a pen and paper (or digital note taking device) handy in case inspiration strikes when you least expect it.

What if you have no idea at all about what to do? Sometimes we are clueless about what we need to do next to make our vision happen, so nothing makes sense. If this is the case for you, here are a few tips to get some clarity and start moving forward.

1. Write Down the Steps You Can See

You don't need to have every single step planned from the beginning of a major project. Just write down the steps you know you can take right now.

My good friend Taylor Call had a vision to create an alliance whose mission would be to create environmentally friendly professional sports teams, venues, and events worldwide. This was a huge idea that would have an equally huge impact. The amount of garbage generated at just one professional sporting event can be greater than that of a large town; not to mention the energy consumption. By getting professional sports teams to adopt a commitment to being 100% eco-conscious organizations, the impact on the health and well-being of the environment would be enormous.

How on earth was she going to do it? This is a billion-dollar idea that involves literally hundreds of thousands of people and the cooperation of rival teams to work together. She had no idea how this was going to come to pass, but what she did know was that she could take small steps to move in the right direction. One immediate step was to register the website name she was given in her vision. So she registered the name greensportsalliance.org.

She began talking to small groups of individuals and held on to the idea that someone would come forward with the ability to make this vision a reality, and do so quickly and successfully.

One day she received a call from an individual who wondered why she had the domain name he wanted. He explained he had the same vision, almost word for word, and was representing someone who already owned several professional sports teams and had the power and influence to move this idea from vision to reality immediately. Since then, GSA has become one of the most influential environmental organizations worldwide with hundreds of professional sports teams, venues, athletes, and of course thousands of fans... and it all started with a big vision and small steps. So write down your next step and take it, even if it's as small as registering the domain name.

2. Ask for Help

You don't need to know everything! There are over seven billion people on the planet and someone will have the answers you need. More often than not, that person is someone you already know. Maybe they even live in the same house as you, or they are a friend on Facebook. Maybe a Google search can give you all you need to know. Maybe you know someone who knows someone who can help you. Ask around, be open to wonders, and see what magic occurs. You are only five people away from anyone in the world.

3. Take a Break

How many times have you given up on something and *then* the answer came? Often, when we are stressing out and forcing things to happen, the Resistance and stress we are feeling blocks our creative mind from working properly. The tension shuts down our genius. One of the best things you can do is get out and go for a walk. Take a long break and try NOT to focus on what you need to do. Focus on something else. Enjoy nature. Breathe deeply. Move your body. Very often you'll discover the answers come flooding in. Take the time to get away and see what happens. Remember: let go. *Fully* let go. Give up on trying to discover anything and just let it happen.

4. Find a Mentor or Training Program

Probably the most effective way to figure out how to get where you want to go is to get help from those who have gone there before. We created Awakened Academy after hundreds of people asked, "How do you break out of a job and do what you love? How do you write and publish a book? How do you awaken spiritually? How do you find out what you're here to do in this world?" To answer all these questions, we created a training program designed to help people who have a mission get going on their mission and succeed.

If you're struggling to work it out on your own, invest in your success and get the support you need. It's the secret to success. The most successful people in the world have invested in their education, mentoring, and coaching. If you're serious about success, find the right support, guidance, and mentors for you and get started, even if it means saving up money to pay for it.

So get the outline of your plan done and then we can move forward into the next phase: making sure you do it!

The blunt reality is having a plan means nothing if you don't do anything with it. Plenty of people have ideas and even a plan yet very few actually bring them to life. You may have already had a plan before you even read this book but...

THE BIG CHALLENGE NOW IS TAKING ACTION

The rest of this book is specifically designed to move you from someone who has dreams to someone who takes massive action and makes things happen!

W H A C K : THE A— ABSOLUTE ACCOUNTABILITY

Pay close attention to this chapter because it contains a key to overcoming procrastination forever and getting going on your mission with full force. This method, if applied correctly, can create nothing short of miracles in your life. On the other hand, if you fail to implement this method, you are unlikely to overcome your own self-sabotage and will probably carry on doing the same old things, over and over again, and stay stuck where you are... or even going backward.

Be warned, while it's easy to start, it's so powerful that it'll probably freak your ego out. In fact, if it doesn't freak you out (at least a little) you've not done it right. The sure sign that big changes are on the horizon are excitement and trepidation. You know you've "got it" when you begin to feel like you're going on an adventure into a new country or a place you've never been before. It is fun and scary at the same time.

HOW I DISCOVERED THIS METHOD

Like most creative entrepreneurs, I've struggled with self-sabotaging habits that dwarfed my achievements and held me in limitation. It seemed any time I started to move forward toward success in a project or in my life, procrastination and perfectionism would abruptly appear in front of me and kick my ass so hard I'd abandon what I was doing and end up wasting vast swaths of my precious life wading about in BS, getting nowhere and losing hope.

Like most creative people, I love starting new things. I'd easily start my projects and move toward my goals, but sooner or later, as things began to move toward completion, my inner teenager, the voice of procrastination and Resistance, would show up and undermine my ability to stay the course. I'd be nearing the end of a project, just about to get it out into the world when a lazy, abusive, spoiled teenager would move into my head and cause a ruckus.

He'd thunder into my mind, put his feet up on my desk, scatter my papers all over the floor, and smash my computer to pieces. Then he would proceed to tell me, in no uncertain terms, to f*ck off. "I'm not interested in your stupid ideas," he'd say. "I've got no time for this sort of sh*t. You can go screw yourself if you think I'm going to help you."

And that was that. My success streak would come crashing to a halt. The ego had kicked in. Again. And I'd be back in procrastination land, trapped in tedious nonsense, obsessively checking my email, spacing out on Facebook, buying more stuff I don't need on Amazon, drifting in and out of random videos and movies, putting out fires, and pretending to be busy doing low-value work that achieved nothing.

I don't know what your inner voice of Resistance tells you, but it's probably not poetry.

Luckily, one day, after years of ups and downs, I discovered a simple little trick that changed everything. It felt as if I'd discovered the Holy Grail or a magic pill to achieve immortality. With this little trick I was able do the impossible: once and for all I was finally able to overcome that annoying voice and self-sabotage mechanism that had ruined my life.

Instead of having part of my psyche fighting with my ideas and intentions, all parts of my inner world were actually cooperating. At last, I felt as if my entire being was aligned with one single aim and going in the same direction. It was like the warring parties had decided to team up and serve the common good instead of bickering among themselves.

The civil war inside me had ended and I was at peace. What an amazing feeling. It was a miracle. The difference from one day to the next was so radical it seemed as if the teenager in my head, the voice of Resistance who had been terrorizing me for years, had been magically transformed overnight. As the new day dawned, I awoke with a sense of wholeness, ease, grace, and peace, coupled with the power and energy to make anything I wanted to happen in real life.

When this first happened, I was shocked and surprised. I felt as if I'd won the lottery and moved into a new world. My only concern was I didn't think it would last. Surely, it couldn't be this good, could it?

After using this magic trick for a while I realized it actually wasn't just a fad, nor was it a fluke—it wasn't even really a magic trick. What I'd discovered was a solid method that actually achieved results, day in and day out. Since that day, I've been able to get things done, finish projects, and make things happen. As long as I stick to the method and don't allow that teenager to return and run the show, things are smooth.

I'm literally surrounded by the positive results of my past actions since I've started using this method. I'm sitting here overlooking a beautiful tropical rain forest, surrounded with amazing white sandy beaches, in the middle of the Pacific Ocean, doing what I love in my beautiful, spacious home, helping countless people all over the world, and getting paid handsomely for it.

If it weren't for this method that has given me the ability to take action and overcome procrastination, I'd not be here today. I'd still be stuck in a little gloomy room feeling depressed.

So what is this magic power? This magic power is commonly known as accountability.

When you are accountable for something, it means you are willing to take complete responsibility for your actions and decisions *and* you are willing and required to pay the consequences of your actions. In other words, if you are accountable, there are no more excuses, and the buck stops with you and *you alone*.

You're about to learn a specific method that creates non-negotiable accountability for yourself so that you can take massive action and achieve remarkable results in your life and business.

FOUR STEPS TO ROCK-SOLID, BULLETPROOF ACCOUNTABILITY:

1. Clarify the results or outcome you want to achieve (your vision and plan).

2. Set up an **external influence** to hold you accountable for taking those actions and achieving results.

3. Expose your actions and results to that external influence with complete transparency and integrity.

4. Pay any consequences of your actions.

An important word in setting up accountably is *external.* You are accountable to an external, outside influence for your actions and results—not an *internal* influence. In other words, you are not just accountable to yourself, but to someone else.

THE IMPORTANCE OF HAVING EXTERNAL INFLUENCES HOLDING YOU ACCOUNTABLE

Why can't you just be accountable to yourself? For years I felt that I should be able to do everything I wanted to do on my own without any help from anyone else. My reasoning was that anything I really wanted to do was my choice and my responsibility. Therefore, if I wanted to do it, I would. My mind would say things like: "I can make this happen on my own! I don't need any help from anyone. I don't like involving anyone else. It's my project so it's up to me to do it!" My "spiritual" ego protested the idea of accountability by saying things like, "I don't need any human beings to help me; I'm too spiritual for that. I can do it with God; I can rely on my spiritual power or higher self."

This Resistance to external accountability is common in entrepreneurs and creators. Many of us who go out on our own to make things happen are proud, independent, stubborn people who don't like to involve others in our creative process, and certainly don't like to be told what to do. We love our freedom and will often fight to the death to maintain it. That's one of the main reasons we become entrepreneurs in the first place. We quit our jobs so we could be our own bosses, do what we want, and live on our own schedule, free of external accountability and being told what to do. But this so-called freedom and lack of external accountability ultimately and routinely backfires on us.

Without anyone to answer to except ourselves, our Resistance creeps in. Without our being aware of what is happening we start to create long lists of clever excuses to keep us stuck in our limitations while this sabotaging part of us convinces us that we are heroes who can do everything on our own. This warped sense of freedom and false sense of pride is our downfall. If we're not careful, we will be fooled by our clever self-sabotage and waste our lives away as slaves to our limited thinking while simultaneously believing we are free.

After enough failure and self-sabotage, I finally became humble enough to realize I had a big ego and ruthless Resistance and I simply couldn't do this all on my own. If I could have, I would already have been doing it. If you could do everything you wanted to, you'd already be doing it, but you aren't. As long as we're left to our own warped thinking, we'll be stalling, wading around in BS, and getting nowhere.

YOUR OWN MIND HAS FAILED YOU

Your inner voice has been lying to you. You really do need support to succeed if you want to achieve something important and meaningful in life.

Accountability is powerful because it abruptly removes the seductive excuses and makes certain you get the results you say you want. Accountability overcomes the unconscious behaviors, the laziness and subtle games we play with ourselves to wiggle our way out of doing what really matters to us.

Accountability helps us get clear about what we need to do so that we can do it *now.* And then keep doing it every day.

Accountability is about integrity. It's about aligning our thoughts, words, and actions. Accountability is about putting your money where your mouth is and being the real deal. Accountability is your key to freedom. In order for it to work, you need to set it up right.

By now, you know what you're accountable for. The next step is to clearly and consciously create the consequences you face for not doing what you know you want to do. This is where the rubber meets the road and you turn your dreams into a tangible reality. You can know this is a good idea in your head, but actually doing it requires a serious commitment.

CONSEQUENCES:
THE SECRET TO GETTING IT DONE

When we are not living the life we were meant to live, there is a serious price to pay. Procrastinating, slacking off, getting distracted, drifting, and disempowering ourselves has painful consequences. When we're not doing what we know we should be doing with our lives, we suffer a little more each day. Every day we postpone doing what we need to do, we are slipping backward further into depression, boredom, and mediocrity.

Before you set up accountability, it's essential to realize you are already 100% accountable for your life. You are already getting the consequences of your thoughts, words, and actions. It's already happening. When we're screwing around and rolling about in horse crap, our life is miserable. We pay the price of wasting our precious time by denying ourselves the joy of life. When we're not doing what we need to do, we're already ruining our future and setting ourselves up for a life of drama and more BS, boredom, depression, and failed dreams.

The consequences of many things we do in life are not immediate, so we can carry on being slack for months, years, or even decades before we finally have to face our problems. Let's take our diet for example. Eating junk food won't kill you right away. It normally feels quite good for a little while. But if we keep eating junk day after day, year after year, we'll end up with some kind of disease. Using a credit card won't destroy your finances right away, but over time, as the interest keeps piling up, you will find yourself drowning in a sea of debt.

Ironically, setting up external accountability is the best way not to need external accountability. Why? If we do things that ruin our lives, we will end up bankrupt, sick, depressed, and lost. We may even end up in jail or facing problems in our community. Once any of these things happen, we require external factors to control us or pull us out of our problems. By setting up accountability, we avoid problems before they begin and make certain we are successful. We avoid future challenges and free ourselves of the need to have external factors dictating our lives.

With accountability we don't let another year slide by before we feel the pain of our actions. We choose to create self-empowered situations where we feel the pain of our actions right away. We choose to set things up so we pay a price for avoiding life and making mistakes now, instead of getting into debt with ourselves and paying for it later. Accountability is the ultimate form of self-respect and personal responsibility. By setting up accountability, we're closing the gap between our actions and the impact they have on us so we can accurately gauge where we are now.

Accountability is like preventative medicine. Once we can see the problems we will face in the future if we don't change, we will choose to fix those problems before they get any worse, starting now.

Accountability means setting up clearly defined artificial consequences for ourselves when we make mistakes. Instead of letting ourselves get away with abandoning our goals, we give *ourselves* a slap on the wrist through whatever means necessary.

For example, I have a list of things I'm committed to doing each day. If I don't do these things, the consequence I've set up is that I have to pay $100 to someone. The real consequence of my screwing up and avoiding life is far greater than losing $100, but the $100 acts as a reminder to my ego that there are real consequences for not making things happen.

My ego doesn't want to lose $100 every day it slacks off, so this small consequence helps those sabotaging elements of my psyche get on board and do what is needed.

The number you pay each day could be changed, or you may not want to use money at all. The whole point of setting up accountability is to create clear consequences for your actions that will freak out your inner teenager and enable you to do what you need to do.

Accountability is designed to destroy Resistance and encourage action. That's all. Whatever you need to set up for yourself so that you'll do the things you need to do is great. You'll know it's working when you're able to do things that you were not able to do before.

WHO IS ACCOUNTABILITY FOR?

There are various aspects of our psyche. Our higher self, or our genius, doesn't need accountability. There is a big part of us that already wants to succeed and is more than happy to make things happen. Accountability and consequences are set up exclusively for that spoiled, lazy bastard in your head who needs to be threatened to cooperate and will resist unless he's put under pressure.

When I first thought of writing this book, my working title was "Fining the Inner Teenager," because the whole point of accountability is to get that lazy bastard on board by using a language it understands—tangible penalties or being grounded.

My own inner teenager doesn't like the idea of handing over $100 to someone—so once he's told to "cooperate or lose $100," he'll humor me and let the important things I need to do happen. It may seem strange and even a little immature for us to need this, but the fact is, it works. This part of us called the inner teenager, the ego, the lower self, or whatever description you prefer, is obsessed with limited pleasures, money, fame, looking good, and being liked by others. So we need to use these consequences to make sure that part of us stops blocking our success and gets on board with what's needed.

After a period of taking action, those important new habits and projects become ingrained in unconscious ways of being that result in success.

The $100 threat to the ego has turned an enemy into an ally.

If you're thinking, "No way! I'm not going to put down $100 per day to be accountable to someone else. I need my money," it's a good sign your ego is afraid. You've understood what's at stake here.

If you don't have any emotional reaction from this, it means it hasn't sunk in yet. But by the time we get to the end of this chapter, it will have.

"But I don't want to do it because of money." Many people resist the idea of having punishments or doing things because of the money. They think, "Why don't I just set up a reward for myself instead of a punishment?"

Other people say things like, "I'm not a dog! I don't need to be motivated by rewards or punishment." But they are missing the point.

PAY VERY CLOSE ATTENTION HERE

The part of you that's already excited about life and wants to make things happen doesn't need any accountability at all. That part of you is also not motivated by rewards. There is a pure essence within us that's already excited, motivated, and ready to do what's right for us. Accountability is not designed to get *that* aspect of us on board. Accountability is a means of keeping your ego in check. It's a method designed to stop the self-sabotaging monster inside us from ruining our lives and destroying our will to do what we need to do. That's all.

Whenever I tell people about "forced consequences" and "punishments," almost everyone's ego reacts and rebels. They normally say something like: "I don't want any consequences. I want to do it from the heart, not because of fear or punishment," or "I don't want to do accountability, it doesn't FEEL right to me."

I totally understand. We all want to do what's right for us from the heart and not because of external events. We don't want to be forced into action or pay the price for being slack. Of course, I get it. I feel the same way.

But pay close attention. How successful are you?

How's that working for you?

Be honest here. Are you doing what you want to do?

Or are you under-achieving?

You're reading this book because your life is not as good as you want, isn't that right?

You don't have the success you want, do you?

Be humble....

If you're honest, you'll probably agree that your current methods to make things happen have failed.

Doing it "from the heart" hasn't worked, has it?

Why not?

It hasn't worked because your ego, your lower self, is currently more powerful than your heart. It rules your heart. In other words, your heart already says, "YES! I WANT TO DO IT! I don't need any accountability."

But then your ego, the lazy, selfish teenager says, "Screw you! I'm not doing it! No way!"

And who normally wins?

If your heart were winning you wouldn't be reading this book! If you could already do it from the heart, you would be. You're reading this because the lower self has sabotaged your life.

Let's get something super clear. Your heart is ALWAYS on board with your best interests. YOU already want to do this from the heart. Accountability is not for your heart to get on board. Accountability is ONLY for the ego or lower self to get on with it. Your lower self is never going to do anything from the heart. It doesn't give a flying fart about the heart.

That's why we need to help this lower part of us get on board by creating methods that work at that level. You can't reason with fanatical terrorists. They will kill you. You can't tell them to come from the heart. They will cut off your head. There is no reasoning with a madman.

There is no reasoning with your lower self. It's out to screw you up.

Accountability is about creating a situation where your heart can thrive and not be sabotaged by the terrorism of the lower self. There is a war going on inside each of us. The battle is won only by realizing we have these darker parts of ourselves and by strengthening the heart.

We will never get anywhere in life if we are constantly unable to do what's going to give us strength.

Realize clearly that accountability is not about force and suppression. It's about being humble and doing what is needed to get the results we need. I've seen people do amazing things with accountability.

ACCOUNTABILITY IS A SIGN OF SELF-LOVE AND SELF-RESPECT

If you had a terrorist in your house, would you say, "Sure, do what you want! Take my house, my money, my car, and all my stuff! I don't mind if you kill me and my family. That's fine." Or would you stand up to protect your family?

What we have to realize is the "punishment" of giving the ego a fine for not showing up is nothing compared to the real punishment of being ruled by our ego and having a crappy life we hate.

So before you throw this away, ask yourself: do I want to be ruled by my lower self and live a boring life? Or do I want to get the annoying thing on board so I can create freedom, wealth, abundance, and joy?

HOW TO SET UP ACCOUNTABILITY SO YOU BECOME A RESULTS MAGNET

Like most things in life, not all accountability is made equal. Some forms of accountability create remarkable results while other types crash and burn. If you want to become a results magnet and create remarkable things in your life, it's critical you take your time to set this up right. This simply means it works for you. I'll do my best to guide you through the method to figure it out, but ultimately, only you can get this right.

You'll know you've "got it" when you feel excited, energized, and also a little fearful. Excitement and energy naturally emerges because you've opened the door to a new chapter in your life. Along with this, you are likely to also experience some level of fear, like having butterflies in your stomach before you walk out onto a stage to perform. This tingling unease is a sign that, on a deeper level, you are truly committed and you really mean business.

By noticing how you feel, you can tell if this has really sunk in or registered with you, or if it's just a nice idea that you have no real intention of following. Keep refining your accountability until you feel genuinely excited and notice a sense of newness and change in your life.

The method for setting up accountability effectively has six main components. Let's take them one at a time.

Step 1: What Do You Want to Achieve?

Hopefully, you already know what you want to achieve in the next 21 days and have written it down clearly. If not, go back to the previous sections and do it! Knowing what you want gives you the power of focus and allows you to stay the course and get results. If you don't know what you want to do, how can you be accountable to do it?

You'll know you've picked something meaningful to you when you feel strong and excited about it.

There are two different, but connected types of accountability, and I suggest you set them both up.

1. What specific results are you accountable to achieve by the end of the month?

Example: I will finish my book by May 30th.

2. What specific actions will you be accountable to take every day in order to achieve these results?

Example: I will write in my book or do other work related to my book for two hours every day.

Let's get clear on each type of accountability.

1. Accountability for Your Specific End Result

What is the big outcome you want to achieve by the end of the month?

This will probably be easy. It's simply the end result or final outcome you desire. For example, to *finish my book* or *to launch my product.*

Within the next 21 days, I am accountable to _____

_____(End Result)

2. Your Daily Accountability

What specific actions are most likely to propel you toward achieving your big goal?

If you are writing a book, for example, then sitting down to write every day is probably going to be the main thing. No writing, no book.

If you're launching a podcast, creating your audios and preparing for your launch are likely to be the most important things for you to do. Daily accountability is designed to help ensure you do whatever you need to do in order to succeed.

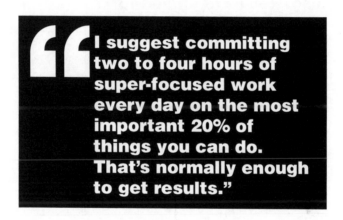

> "I suggest committing two to four hours of super-focused work every day on the most important 20% of things you can do. That's normally enough to get results."

We'll talk more about your top 20% activities later on. For now, simply get clear on what main type of work will help you move forward every day.

What are you going to be accountable to achieve?

> Every day, I will _____
>
> _____ for _____ hours.

Remember: you only need to set up accountability for the ONE MAIN THING that will have the greatest positive impact on everything else. There's no point in making yourself accountable to breathe or brush your teeth unless you want to start consciously breathing deep or brushing your teeth more often. Get this clear and make sure you feel good about it before you move onward.

Step 2: Write Down Your Accountability Contract

Your success rests on getting this part right. Slow down and take the time to figure this out. Stay with it until you're totally clear and ready to jump into it. I recommend you write your answers down in a digital document of some kind so you can edit and change it as needed and also so you can send it to your accountability partner for review.

Consequences: What Will Happen If You Do Not Do the Things You Have Agreed To?

You may agree to pay $100 per day if you do not do the things you agreed to do. I find money is often the most effective because the ego doesn't like to lose money.

If you're going to set up accountability for money, you can either give money to your accountability partner every day you don't show up, or you can give money to a third party, such as a charity, every time you don't show up. I personally prefer giving money to a third party, because if I am giving money to my accountability partner, they might be inclined to want me to fail. It's very subtle, but I prefer to avoid it.

Here is an example of a specific money-based accountability:

I commit to writing my book for two hours every day. If I don't do it, I'll pay

$100 to _____ per day that I don't write.

If money is not involved, then what else could you agree to do when you don't show up for your accountability? What would your ego want to avoid?

What About Rewards Instead of Punishments?

If you want to offer yourself a reward for doing something instead of an unpleasant consequence, then you can create something like this.

I commit to writing my book for two hours every day. If I do it, I'll buy myself a gift. If I don't do it, I'll get nothing.

Consider this carefully because each of us is different and whatever you create needs to work for you. Generally speaking, rewards don't work as well as negative consequences, but at the end of the day, the only thing that counts is if you're doing what you want to do. While attending a conference, I met the owner of a highly successful vegan cookie company who had used a fascinating form of accountability to get his business off the ground. Before he started his business, he'd been unemployed and living with other unemployed homeless people drifting through the years and getting nowhere. He knew what he needed was a good kick in the pants to snap him out of his situation, so here's what he did.

One day, while holding a can of dog food, he announced to his fellow drifters, he was going to set up a successful cookie company and make over one million dollars in sales by the end of the year. If he had not set it up and not made a million dollars in sales one year from that day, he would eat this can of dog food in front of them.

Being a vegan, he couldn't think of anything worse than eating dog food in front of his friends. And guess what... a year later his company had made a million dollars. At the time of writing, The Alternative Baking Company is still going strong.

But wait! Before you start searching for dog food or some other nasty thing to eat, make sure that you stop and think about what's going to work for you, personally. What will inspire you to take massive action? What do you want to avoid?

The reason accountability can work so well is the ego wants to avoid pain, humiliation, and paying a price, and would prefer to cooperate with you doing your work than give up or lose something. So take the time to get creative and come up with a consequence that you're 100% certain will be effective enough to get all parts of you to take action. Whatever you need to do for it to work, do that. There are no rules here. Setting up your consequences correctly is absolutely essential to your success.

What Is Your Consequence for Not Achieving Your Goal?

Write it down.

How Will You Communicate Your Results to Your Accountability Partner?

Clear communication is critical, otherwise your accountability can become obsolete or over-complicated and you won't be able to sustain it. If it's too vague, then you may as well not bother at all. If it's too complicated, you can cause unnecessary Resistance. There are many ways to communicate with your accountability partner. Choose a method that is easy and sustainable for you.

- Will you email them every day?
- Will you text them?
- Will you talk to them personally?
- Will you call or Skype them?

The main thing is to make certain that whatever you agree to is clear and there is no room for confusion or mixed messages.

Here's a good example of clear accountability for the above questions:

Every evening I will text my accountability partner Zoe before 8 PM that "I wrote for two hours today." If I don't text, or I write less than two hours, I'll pay the consequence by sending $100 to XYZ charity.

This is clear communication because it includes:

- WHEN you will do it (evening)
- HOW you will communicate (text)
- WHO you will connect with (your accountability partner—we'll get to this later)
- WHAT you did
- THE CONSEQUENCE of what you did

An example of vague accountability could look like this:

I'll tell ZOE what I did. (When? How? How often?)

Or

If I do what I wanted to do, I'll let ZOE know about it.

Vague communication leads to lack of focus and poor results. Do yourself a massive favor and get clear on exactly what you are going to achieve.

When Will You Begin and End This Accountability?

It's wise to establish a clear, meaningful beginning and end date for your accountability.

- What date will your accountability begin?
- When will it end?
- Are there any exceptions?

   For example:

   I will do _____

   _____ every day except when I'm traveling.

   I will do _____

   _____Monday-Friday.

How Will You Know You're Done?

You'll know you're ready when you end up with something like this, written clearly in a form that you can send to your accountability partner:

From May 1st until June 1st, I Michael Mackintosh, commit to write in my book every day for at least two hours. I will text my accountability partner (Name) every day before I go to bed to let them know if I did it or not, by saying, "I wrote in my book for X number of hours today."

If I don't do it, or if I don't text them, I will give $100 to ACME Charity via PayPal. To prove I've made the payment, I will send my accountability partner a copy of the receipt in an email for each day I miss.

Final Accountability

1. Accountability for Your Big Result

I _____ (your name)

Commit to _____

_____ (specific result)

By _____

I will _____ (email, text, call)

If I fail to achieve this result, I will pay _____

_____

_____(how much $ or what other things you will do)

2. Daily Accountability

Starting (date) _____

Ending (date) _____

I _____ (your name)

Commit to doing _____ (what)

For _____ (how long)

I will _____ (text, email, call, see)

_____ (Who)

And tell them _____ (What)

If I don't do it, or don't contact them, I will _____

_____(what is your consequence)

BOOM! Congratulations! From here on out, it's all fun and games! Now all you need is to find the right person who will be happy to work with you on this!

Step 3: Choosing Your Accountability Partner

Here's what to look for in a great accountability partner:

- They have your best interests at heart.

- They are willing and happy to participate and to get a message every day from you via email, Facebook, or text, etc., saying you did the things you're accountable to do, or you didn't.

- They will firmly HOLD YOU ACCOUNTABLE if you don't get back to them or start making excuses. This is important because if they don't hold you accountable, the agreement is meaningless.

- Bonus Blessing: they are someone you don't want to disappoint.

Consider the above and pick your accountability partner. CONTACT THEM RIGHT NOW. Seriously. Stop everything and contact them. If they are available, go to them physically; go see them and tell them what you're doing and set up your accountability. If they're not physically with you, then phone, text, or email them right now. Let them know what you're doing and set up your accountability.

Go do it right now. Secret cameras have been installed to check if you're doing this or not. You have been warned! Come back here once you've set it all up. We're watching you!

Step 4: Busting Your "Inner Wiggler"

Chances are your accountability has "wiggle room" that will weaken your resolve to make miracles happen. We need to fix that. Your inner wiggler is the part of you that will wiggle its way out of accountability by making your commitment vague, by lying, by bending facts, by making the consequences unreliable, or by choosing someone who won't hold you accountable.

For this magic power to work in your life, you need to overcome your inner wiggler's games by foreseeing them and solving potential wiggling before it happens.

Here Are a Few Tips for Removing All the Wiggle Room That Will Sabotage Your Success:

1. Make sure your accountability partner knows exactly what the deal is and is 100% on board with what you're doing. If they are not happy with the idea of being your accountability partner, or they secretly want you to fail, it's better to find someone else.

2. Give them some money or whatever the consequence is IN ADVANCE so you can't wiggle out of it.

3. Have a super clear list of what you are supposed to do on the wall next to your bed or somewhere you can see it so that every day you can check off what you do or don't do.

4. Don't make it too hard. Just add one to two important new things you need to do. Make the actual agreement something you are capable of doing.

5. Make it super clear whether you did the things or not. For example, did you do 20 minutes of exercise or not? Time yourself. Keep it clear and specific.

What else could trip you up? What other things need to be upgraded so this really works? Take the time now to refine your agreement until there is no wiggle room left to fail.

Don't just think about this. Actually do it!

Step 5: Make a Public Commitment

"I made a commitment to completely cut out drinking and anything that might hamper me from getting my mind and body together. And the floodgates of goodness have opened upon me—spiritually and financially."

— DENZEL WASHINGTON

Making a public commitment to do what you want to do adds extra fuel to your accountability fire. Once we realize we're up against a stubborn ego that wants the opposite of what we want, it becomes clear we may as well use everything we can to get where we want to go.

Here's why making a public commitment works so well. Our society is able to function on the basis of trust. We believe that most people will do what they say most the time. If we didn't have this foundation, we'd be afraid to drive, would never bother to make appointments, send letters, or try to cooperate with anyone. We are social beings and we don't feel comfortable letting people down or breaking our promises.

Public humiliation is many people's greatest fear, and we'll do almost anything to avoid being disapproved of by our tribe. This is why so many of us are scared to death of public speaking or putting our work out into the world. Once we "get out there" our ego is afraid that we could be hated, heckled, or even killed. Of course, that doesn't normally happen, but this built-in fear of being humiliated is enough to freak us out and keep us from doing the things we know we should do.

So how can we use this psychological principle to our advantage?

Connected to fear of humiliation is our need to be consistent with what we say. If we tell people whom we admire that we'll do something, it's socially unacceptable to break our word. We are, quite literally, held to our word through the force of public commitment and our fear of letting people down. To break our word would mean disappointing people, acting without integrity, and being seen as untrustworthy—all of which could lead to bad things happening to us. We could lose our job, destroy a relationship, or be excluded from certain privileges and opportunities.

So to fuel the fire of our determination and accountability, we can use this need to be consistent to our advantage.

The ego loves to be praised and hates to be seen as a failure or be told we're bad. The ego wants to avoid humiliation. So when we make public commitments to other people we admire, we engage the part of us that doesn't want to be humiliated. Once a public commitment is made, that lazy teenager who "couldn't give a sh*t" five minutes ago suddenly jumps into action in order to save face. Instead of resisting, the lower part of us is now motivated to cooperate.

How Can You Set up a Public Commitment That Will Activate Your Will to Succeed?

The ego is more affected by bigger and more serious things. So the more public your announcement, as in the more people who know what you are doing, or the more influential those people are, the more likely you will follow through on your word.

The more pressure you can put on yourself the better. Again, don't get all emotional and sentimental on me and say, "Oh, but I don't like pressure, I just do it from the heart. I'll just do it for me; I don't care what others think." Maybe you don't care, and I believe you are already coming from the heart. But your ego does care about humiliation and your ego will try every trick in the book to avoid doing what you want to do. Your ego is what's stopping you from getting things done. So, while doing things from your heart and for yourself is fine in theory, it doesn't work if you're not actually doing all those things, does it?

I just got back from the beach where I met a friend who used to be a client. She cancelled her coaching with me as soon as the rubber met the road and I encouraged her to take action and actually get her work out. Three years have passed, and now, after a two-hour conversation and lots of love, commitments, and coaching, she has finally committed to creating one video! A huge step in the right direction toward her dreams. And only a few years later. Better late than never. By making a public commitment to Arielle and me, she is far more likely to actually do it.

Making a public commitment helps you overcome your ego and your own inner monsters that are on a mission right now to sabotage you.

Do you want to finally destroy procrastination and bring your ideas to life? Do you want an awesome life? Do you want to live your life or hide from it?

Let's do it.

1. Write Your Commitment

Make it as clear and powerful as possible so you can't wiggle out of it, and so you'll unconsciously feel compelled to make it happen.

Here is a basic template.

I _____ (your name)

Commit to completing this _____

_____ (project, practice, book, etc.)

by _____ (give a date).

Signed _____ (your name)

Date _____

Once you've done this you'll have something like this:

I, Michael Mackintosh, commit to completing the first draft of this book, by Jan 1, 2018.

Signed: Michael Mackintosh

Date: 12/09/2017

2. Put It Where You Can See It

Stick this on your wall next to your bed or near your desk where you can't miss it.

3. Burn Your Bridges and Your Boats!

Take it a step further and make it really happen. Go onto Facebook and other social media websites you are connected to and make an announcement that you're going to do whatever you're doing. Yes, this is where it gets real.

Cut and paste your commitment. You can rephrase it a little so it's less formal, but make it clear.

For example:

Hey everyone, as of today I'm going to be doing _____

_____

for 21 days. Hold me accountable. I am 100% committed to this.

Or:

Today I started my new project to _____

_____.

I will have it finished by _____. Stay tuned for more.

4. Tell People You Admire

Write your commitment to 10 people you respect and who'll feel disappointed if you don't do it. Send them all a short message about what you're doing and when it will be done. You can do this in an email, via social media, or you can physically give them a card or mail something to them. Let them know that you're telling them to hold you accountable because you admire them.

I heard a story of a woman who gave up smoking after 20 years simply by writing: "I have stopped smoking" on a card and giving it to her top 10 most influential people. She couldn't give smoking up for herself, but she didn't want to let them down. So with that simple task, she completely stopped smoking.

The more you respect and appreciate these particular people and don't want to let them down, the more powerful this will be.

Okay, so now you know what to do. Go make your commitments and share the good news far and wide.

What Will Happen When You Make a Commitment?

Once you make a true commitment in your heart and soul with determination, you evoke higher powers. You attract the muse to inspire you and your life becomes magical. You also set into motion strange and unseen forces to support your mission and tests to challenge your resolve that will bring out the best in you.

Commit now.

CHAPTER 16

WHACK: THE C— CONDITIONS & STRUCTURES

ORGANIZING YOUR LIFE FOR SUCCESS

I want to congratulate you for getting this far. You are awesome. You can expect big changes in your life now. If you didn't do any of the previous steps, go back and do them! Seriously. Each step is extremely potent and will allow you to magically create huge upgrades in your life. I'm excited for you. Now, all that remains is how to most effectively take action to make your goals happen.

Conditions and structures refer to the scaffolding we set up in order to make things happen in 21 days. This means consciously designing our life to remove friction and make it as easy as possible for us to do the things we need to do.

You've already done part of this by:

1. Knowing what you want

2. Setting up accountability

3. Making a commitment

Now let's focus on how you can more efficiently do the things you need to do so you will achieve your goals on time.

WHAT ARE CONDITIONS AND STRUCTURES?

Conditions and structures are the situations, objects, and rituals you need to set up so it's EASY for you to do the things you need to do. Let's look at an example.

How to Set up Conditions and Structures For a Daily Green Smoothie

Imagine you wanted to have a green smoothie every day. It might seem as if not much thought is required to make this happen, but if you don't have the right ingredients to make it, or if your blender is hidden under the cupboard and hard to get out, it's probably not going to happen. Most people say they want to eat better, but they don't. Why not?

The reason for not doing so often seems trivial and can easily be solved with conditions and structures. Setting up the conditions and structures for a smoothie might mean buying all the ingredients you need like bananas, and putting them on the counter or in the fridge. You could also get your blender out of the cupboard and place it somewhere easily accessible so you can't miss it every time you're in the kitchen. Maybe add a note on the fridge to remind you to make it, or better, agree to make a smoothie for someone else who will be waiting for it. Once you've set these things up, when you walk into the kitchen in the morning, everything you need will already be there waiting for you. Grab the blender, add the ingredients, push a button, and you're done.

Why are these little things so important? Because the Resistance is lethal. It's funny how even the smallest deviation from this can screw it all up. I remember for years I wanted to have smoothies every day, but it rarely happened. My special smoothie powders and herbs I liked to add to the smoothies were hidden in the cupboard behind some other stuff. That minor inconvenience (of having to move things out of the way) was enough to make me abandon making a smoothie and eat something else. It seems trivial, but it's not. It sabotaged my smoothie intentions for years!

To remedy this, all I needed to do was grab the tubs of smoothie powders and put them next to the blender and then, like magic, making smoothies every day was easy.

So let's break down the conditions and structures for a smoothie.

Well, let's say your smoothie is made from bananas, greens, water, and smoothie Powders.

It could be more fancy than this—but let's keep it simple for now.

So in order for you to make sure you have your smoothie every day, you need to make sure that you've got all the ingredients in the house at all times and your blender works—otherwise you can't do it. This may sound obvious, but it's not. Lots of people would love to have a green smoothie every morning, but they fail to do the simple steps needed to make sure it's physically possible. So what conditions and structures could you have in place?

Here Are Conditions and Structures That Worked for Us:

1. Get a large quantity of ripe bananas, peel them, and put them in the freezer (so you have frozen bananas ready to go). We have them delivered to us.

2. Make sure you've got a solid supply of greens. We have a local farmer who delivers organic greens to us twice a week.

3. Get your smoothie powder and put it on the counter next to the blender (or somewhere really easy to access).

4. Put the blender somewhere that is super easy to see and use.

5. My wife and I both have smoothies, and one of us is responsible for making them, which radically increases the likelihood we will both have them.

By having these five things in place, it makes having green smoothies every day super easy. Before we set this up, we never got around to having our green smoothies.

I want to make sure you really understand this method, so here are a few more examples to help you really get how strangely simple yet impactful this method can be for you.

Example 1: Conditions and Structures to Finish the First Draft of Your Book

At this point, let's assume you've already told people what you're doing; you've set up accountability and now you just have to do it. What conditions and structures will make it easy to write every day so that you actually finish your book?

Here's what made it easy for me:

At 5:00 a.m., after my meditation, I make a pot of tea (or coffee) and sit at my desk until 7:00 a.m. to write. The early morning writing time allows me to make great strides in my work before daily distractions start bubbling up.

The conditions and structures I need to set up are as follows:

1. Go to bed early (so I can get up early).

2. Put the alarm clock on the floor away from the bed so I have to get out of bed to turn it off.

3. Make tea or coffee.

4. Have a comfortable office and desk with a bright light and music I enjoy.

This may seem simple and obvious, but these little things are far more significant than they initially appear. The reality is if I go to bed late, I won't wake up early. And, even if I do get enough sleep, if I don't have my alarm away from the bed, I'll probably turn it off, and go back to sleep. Either way, if I don't get up early, I'll miss my writing time. If I get up early, I find it more enjoyable and productive to sit down with a nice cup of tea. So making my tea gets me in the mood for writing, as does the music.

So all this added up—plus the accountability and deadlines—allows me to make sure I actually sit my ass down between 5:00 and 7:00 a.m. and write. Otherwise, I wouldn't. I'd get distracted.

The last condition and structure I recommend is specific accountability to finish your book. Writing it is only part of the equation. You can write all you like, reworking the same pages over and over forever, but if you never finish your book, it will never be read. That's why it's so essential to set up some kind of accountability to make sure you do it.

Example 2: Meditate More

A few years back, we wanted to do meditation every night for one to two hours. The problem was we just never did it. We were always too distracted to stop and meditate so it never happened. We realized we needed to set up conditions and structures to make it possible.

Here's what we did: we texted two people to let them know we were doing a meditation in the evening and gave them the time to arrive.

With that ONE step, a simple text message, we miraculously were able to stop, tidy the house, and sit for meditation for two hours, no problem. That's it, one step. One text message. Boom. Job done.

So as you can see, change can be easy with the right conditions and structures in place. In this case, we knew people would be arriving at our house, so we had to be ready.

NOTE: Did you see the commitment and accountability factors at work here?

Example 3: Inspiring Morning Wisdom

To energize my mind and create an enlightened context for my life, I enjoy reading inspired spiritual texts in the morning after meditation. It helps give me perspective on life and allows my day to flow with less stress and more ease. However, for a while I somehow stopped doing it and I began to wonder what was going on. Why had I abandoned something that was so good for me?

At first, I thought I was either lazy or somehow less interested than before. But on closer inspection, I realized something simple and less obvious had happened. After rearranging the furniture one day, it happened that the pile of texts I usually read got moved. This meant that rather than being able to simply reach out and grab something to read while still sitting on my meditation chair, I'd have to get up and walk into another room to get one, and then come back and sit down again. This minor change was enough to disrupt and abruptly end my morning reading routine.

The Solution: I simply moved the things I wanted to read BACK to where they were so I could easily pick them up after meditation. The result? I now continue to read inspiring words of wisdom every morning.

Again, this may sound silly, but it's not. It's human nature. We are creatures of habit acting mostly unconsciously on autopilot. It's good to see the humor in it and call it out for what it is. The slightest change to our environment can lead to significant changes in the quality of our lives. That's why it's wise to design our lives so we can cruise through our day and get the best out of life without thinking too hard, digging for smoothie powder from the back of the cupboard, or having what we need to read be placed in a different room.

Example 4: Avoiding Unhealthy Habits

I've always loved chocolate. In fact, I enjoy it so much I cofounded a successful raw chocolate company in the UK that has now sent millions of OmBar Chocolate bars to chocolate lovers across the world. It's some of the best chocolate I've ever had, and I mean that. However, it really is possible to have too much of a good thing. There was a time when I had so much chocolate around the house that I didn't eat much else. The good news is the chocolate I had was high quality—raw, organic, no dairy, and made with low-glycemic coconut sugar. Even so, living exclusively on chocolate isn't a good idea. The problem was if I saw lovely chocolate bars winking at me all the time, I ate them. It's so tasty and convenient that it was hard to resist, especially because I had so much of it and almost felt it was my obligation to eat it.

Unfortunately, a chocolate diet isn't sustainable. It left me feeling overstimulated and wired.

Rather than having to force myself not to eat it (which is hard), I simply moved the chocolate to a place in my kitchen that was tough for me to reach. What this did was make sure I became conscious of what I was doing every time I reached out for the chocolate instead of unconsciously eating it all day.

This one tiny change of moving the chocolate so that it wasn't so easily accessible immediately made me eat less chocolate. Each time I went into the kitchen, I'd have to move things to find the chocolate, and that little inconvenience allowed me a moment's space to consider my options and make better choices.

You can apply this same principle to other addictive things. In some cases, it's better to remove things completely so you don't even have access to them at all. An alcoholic, for example, is better off having no alcohol in the house than stocking a full bar. The temptation of all that booze calling out is too great to resist. If you're addicted to checking Facebook or email, then get an app like

Freedom or Antisocial that stops you from obsessively checking it. Or delete the Facebook app from your phone to make it easy to stop spending your whole life staring at a black rectangle. One step further would be to simply unplug your internet router and have someone hide your phone. I've personally done both of these things when I've really needed to focus and get things done.

HOW TO SET UP CONDITIONS AND STRUCTURES FOR *YOUR SUCCESS*

What do you need to add in your life? What do you want to remove from your life? You may want to create a new daily habit, or you may be focused on finishing a specific task. Either way, setting up conditions and structures will make it considerably easier and more effective.

Step 1: What Things Need to Be in Place to Make It Easy for You to Be Successful?

Remember, most of these conditions and structures are not hard or complex things. In fact, if anything, they tend to look so simple that you probably wouldn't even consider them. Don't be deceived by this simplicity. The only thing that matters is that it works.

If you find jumping up and down three times and doing a little jig puts you in the right mood to do whatever you need to do, then do it! It doesn't matter how silly or simple these things are. They just need to work.

So what are your conditions and structures? Write them down.

Step 2: What Did You Miss?

Have another look....

Are these conditions and structures going to guarantee your success?

Are they super easy?

Are you super clear on exactly what you need to do?

Write it all down so it's clear and you can set it up easily.

Step 3: Do It *Now*

Before you move on, go and set up your conditions and structures. Buy the thing you need. Set up your life for success. This is your key to freedom...did you do it? Don't read on until you do this!

THE INEVITABLE THINKING STRATEGY: THE SECRET BEHIND THE WHACKING STICK

By now, you know that setting goals and getting clear on what you want is essential to your success.

No goals or aim = drifting.

Drifting = you lose.

You also know that you need daily rituals, conditions, structures, and accountability to succeed.

What you may not have thought much about is what's called **Inevitable Thinking**. This way of thinking is on an even higher level than goal setting and makes 100% certain that your accountability happens. You can think of this as an advanced level accountability that raises the stakes even higher and therefore increases your ability to succeed even more.

By now you may think surely there is nothing more you need to do. This is already intense! And you're right. You may not need this advanced method. But why not go the whole nine yards and create a foolproof system that is guaranteed to work?

Inevitable thinking is about setting up the systems and structures in your life so that SUCCESS BECOMES INEVITABLE. It means setting yourself up so you can't lose.

If you don't do this high-level thinking, you're probably going to get caught and trapped somewhere by the Resistance. There are simply too many things that can slip you up even if you have the greatest allies, and even if you have accountability and daily rituals set up.

So what is inevitable thinking and how does it work in real life to get a project finished? Here's a quick example:

How Winning an Ipad Forced Me to Create a Brand-new, 40-day Audio Training Course *While* Traveling on Vacation

One summer, my wife and I planned a trip to mainland America to get away from our sleepy Kauai paradise island and see some of the best spots in the states. We travelled all over, from Big Sur to Sedona, including San Francisco, Ohio, Texas, Chicago, and Las Vegas. All in all, we took 13 plane rides and had a wonderful trip.

However, three days before we were due to begin our trip, something happened that allowed us to have more fun and also be highly productive at the same time. Just before we left, I listened to a webinar about the power of accountability and inevitable thinking.

The speaker offered a challenge: anyone who could come up with a solid plan to get a new project finished using these methods of accountability would win an iPad. That same day, I was just thinking of getting an iPad so I thought it would be fun to win one. With only about two minutes to conceive of a winning submission, I wrote this:

"I leave for a six-week vacation in three days. My commitment is: I will create a brand-new audio training course while traveling. In the next two days, I'll create a sales page and then set up emails to sell the program while we are on the plane. Then while we're traveling, we'll create the audio program to send to the people who buy it. And to make sure we show up and do it (and not get distracted) we will set up the following:

1. Send an email today telling our people we have a new course coming for them.

2. Tell them that anyone who buys will get DOUBLE their money back if we either miss a day sending it to them or they do not receive the full training course within the time we said we'd have it ready.

So in other words, we are going to use our existing customers to buy the program and then hold us accountable to give it to them. If we screw up, they get $194 each."

The host loved my idea, and I won the iPad right there on the call. A crazy idea...

but it worked. After the call, my wife and I went to the beach to chat about ideas as we had no clue what this course would be about. After some time for reflection, we were inspired to create a relationship course: "How to attract your Soulmate." It's something we could both contribute to and would help a lot of people who did not have their ideal partner.

1. We emailed everyone on our mailing list to tell them a new program was coming soon.

2. We created a sales page with a video and a button to buy.

3. We set up emails to be sent out automatically while we were traveling to sell the training.

4. Then we packed our bags, got on the plane, and off we went to the mainland.

By the time we got off the plane in Los Angeles, we already had tons of signups for the program. Uh oh! Now we had to create this whole training program for people or give everyone who signed up $194 each! With no stable base and with constant travel, this felt like a bit of a stretch, but we were excited nonetheless.

During our trip we recorded most days in our hotel rooms, which was challenging and funny at times. Everyone who joined loved the course. It was a mission with a clear deadline, and we had a lot to lose if we didn't follow through. It pushed us outside our comfort zone, but we did it anyway. Now we have a great training program we can offer for years to come.

We made our success inevitable by setting up clear deadlines and accountability. All the usual excuses no longer mattered. We simply needed to figure out how to do what we needed to do and get on with it. Bottom line: it worked.

We made a simple promise, and our drive to keep that promise forced us to follow through on our goal.

The more you use inevitable thinking to achieve your personal and professional goals, the more you will succeed. Will you just think about this, or will you set yourself up for inevitable success?

When you are ready, turn the page and let's do the last and final step of the WHACK stage so you can knock it out and get it done!

17

WHAC**K**: THE K— KICK-START

CLARIFY THE SPECIFIC ACTIONS TO ACHIEVE YOUR GOALS: BLAST OFF INTO YOUR 21 DAY CHALLENGE

Congratulations, you're becoming a Get It Done ninja! You can do *anything!*

A QUICK RECAP OF WHERE YOU ARE IN THE WHACK SYSTEM

By now you know....

1. W = What You Want to Achieve, Why It's Important, When the Deadline Is, and Where You'll Do It

This is your VISION, your destination.

2. H = How to Do It

This is your step-by-step route to your destination, your PLAN.

3. A = Accountability

You've set up accountability and consequences with a partner.

4. C = Conditions and Structures

You've set these up so it's easy for you to do the things you need to do.

Now it's time to kick-start your project so you can take massive ACTION and bring your ideas to life.

5. K = Kick-Start

In this final part of the WHACK system, you are going to discover precisely what actions you need to take to practically achieve your goals. Once you know this you can kick-start your success and blast off into your 21 day challenge.

Taking action is normally where people (try to) begin. "Just get on with it," they think. "I just need to get off my ass and do my work." As you know, simply trying to take action without these other elements in place often fails miserably. We already know what to do, but we've not been doing it.

It's easy to start, but it's even easier to abandon our vision as soon as the slightest little challenge appears that knocks us off course. This is why, before you can reach your destination, you need to first know where you're going, how you'll get there, and how to set yourself up for success.

So here we are. *Action time.* This where the rubber meets the road as you move forward toward making your visions become tangible realities.

To bring an idea from our mind, the invisible realm of imagination, into the 3D world, we need to set up four things:

1.   **Vision** (what you want to achieve)
2.   **Plan** (the route from where we are now to where we want to be)
3.   **Action** (the tangible, practical steps forward toward our vision)
4.   **Support** (the accountability, conditions, structures, and inevitable thinking)

Imagine you're standing on one side of a vast mountain range. Your vision, your destination, is on the other side of the mountain. Your plan is the map and route you use to travel from where you are now into the future reality, on the other side of the mountain. Your actions are the little steps you take as you move up the mountain, crossing streams, rivers, lush valleys, harsh rock faces, and all the other situations until you finally reach your destination. Your support is your commitment and unbreakable promise to reach the other side no matter what. It's the inner drive and the outer accountability to get there. When you have a burning desire and people are waiting for you on the other side and cheering you on from below, the impossible becomes possible.

Now it's time for you to take action toward your destination, but not just any old action. To be successful we need to know the most potent and effective actions that will lead us directly to our destination.

Not all routes will get you from where you are to the other side of the mountain. If the map is faulty or if you are not careful and fall, you can get completely lost and even die. To die, in this sense, means to get distracted and give up. To get lost means to miss the path and muddle through life as days and weeks go by with little or no result. To get the results you want fast, you need to know the DIRECT path to your goals and then actually step boldly out into the world, come rain or shine, snow or ice.

Some days will be tough and you'll want to give up and run the other way. Some days will feel as if you're flying. The map is not the territory and you never know quite what's going to be thrown at you next, but if you're serious, you'll do it anyway. You'll take massive action, even if it feels awkward, and you'll get where you want to be.

Let's get super clear on what actions will most directly move you toward your success. These are the final keys to making sure you get off your butt and into gear. There's no point in just sitting about looking up at the peak in the distance. We need to take the first step and then the next and the next and the next until we look back and realize we're high up above it all and can't even see where we began. Once you reach that point, you'll be okay. There is no turning back.

DISCOVER YOUR TOP 80/20 ACTIONS

"Vision without execution is hallucination."

— THOMAS EDISON

Let's discover what you'll need to do to get where you want to be. Your actions include all the small stuff, the little steps that lead you along your route to your destination.

Actions are what bring ideas to life. Action means movement, change, and shifts in the 3D world.

As you now know, not all actions are equal. According to the 80/20 rule, about 80% of what we ordinarily do is highly ineffective, like wading about in a boatload of BS. This means you can essentially remove or radically reduce a large amount of what you do and simply focus on the top 20% of activities that actually get results.

If you can replace some of that BS with more of the top 20%, you become radically more effective. The cool thing to remember is these top 20% activities that lead you to success can be done in just a few hours or less per day. So you really *can* do *less* and achieve *more.* But first you need to discover what the most effective things are.

Exercise: Figure out What Top 20% Power-Packed Activities Will Get You Results

1. Turn Your Plan into a List of Action Steps

Look at your Plan for the next 21 days. You know how to do it, but do you know all the smaller steps involved in actually doing it?

Get clarity on the steps now by writing a list of all the action steps you think you need to take to bring your idea to life.

Just get it all down so it's out of your head and onto paper. At this point, don't worry about the order of the steps or getting it all perfect. Just write. Keep writing until everything you know you'll need to do is documented clearly. This might take a while.

Verbs are actions. Your Action List will look something like this:

Phone _____ and talk about _____

_____

Go to _____ and do _____

_____

Email _____

Set up_____

Cancel _____

Install _____

Create _____

Outsource _____

Record _____

Once you've written this all down, let's move on to the next step.

2. What Action Steps Will Give You the Greatest Result With the Least Amount of Work?

Once you've written down all your ideas, find the top 20% that have the greatest RESULT with the least work. Not everything on your list has the same level of impact. To get more done with less work, consider which actions are most likely to get bigger positive results than the rest.

If you're working on a sales presentation to sell your product or service to more people, you should probably start by talking to your potential customers to figure out exactly what they want, what their problems are, and what their ideal solution would look like. Once you've done this kind of market research, it'll make crafting a great presentation that achieves your goal of increasing sales a whole lot easier.

Finding the 20% most effective actions isn't easy. It requires thinking hard instead of working hard. Think smart so you can get better results in less time. What you are looking for are the shortcuts. How can you do less work and take less time, yet move farther along your way?

There are *always* shortcuts in life. We just don't always see them because we're so used to doing things the way we've always done them and don't consider other options.

For example, how many of us get upset by someone and then spend hours, days, weeks, even months or years thinking about the situation? Then eventually you have a straightforward chat with them and clear the whole thing up in just a few minutes? Once we have that "hard conversation" we often wish we'd done it much earlier.

It's also remarkably common to install or upgrade a piece of software and then proceed to waste hours trying to figure out how to do a technical task. Then finally, when we're exhausted and defeated, we give in and ask the right person for help. They fix it for us in five minutes.

It's easy to waste time being stuck and "trying to figure it out." It's your duty as a creator to notice when you're stuck and remove the blocks so you can focus on what you're really here to do and zip up the mountain with as much ease and grace and as little drama as possible.

Exercise: Getting Rid of the Insignificant 80%

1. Look at your complete list of actions and reorder them in the correct sequence from A-Z.

2. What can you remove? Is there anything redundant that you can scratch off the list?

3. What can you outsource?

4. What are the shortcuts?

    Put on your 80/20 consciousness and discover how you can get better results with less effort.

    Upgrade your actions with this in mind. Aim for doing less work, taking less time, and getting a better result. There is always an upgrade

5. Once you're happy with this, rewrite your upgraded TO DO List.

   This is your complete 20% list of everything you need to do to achieve your goal in 21 days.

   Having this level of clarity will bring you peace of mind and joy to your heart. It will inspire you to start making things happen. Once you know your top 20% of actions that matter most, we'll create your weekly 20% list.

6. Break it up into three weekly chunks. You do this by getting clear on the results you want by the end of the each week.

Example:

WEEK 1

RESULTS	ACTION
Book outline done	Write every day from 5:00 to 7:00 a.m. and 8:00 to 11:00 p.m.
5 book chapters done	Research information for the book
Webinar outline done	Talk to clients about the webinar
	Study course on webinars

WEEK 2

RESULTS	ACTION
First draft of book done	Write every day from 5:00 to 7:00 a.m. and 8:00 to 11:00 p.m.
Webinar slides completed	Create webinar slides

WEEK 3

RESULTS	ACTION
Second draft of book done	Write every day from 5:00 to 7:00 a.m. and 8:00 to 11:00 p.m.
Webinar presentation recorded, edited, and ready to launch	Practice webinar presentation
	Ask clients to review the presentation

NOTE: If you can't identify your top 20% activities from the rest, just ignore it for now and stick with your basic list of all the things you need to do. In time, you'll see firsthand which things are the 20% that matter most and which are the 80% that don't have much impact. Pay attention to the actions get will get you the best results.

CHECKLIST: ARE YOU READY TO BEGIN YOUR 21 DAY CHALLENGE?

Make sure you're clear about what you're doing and ready to rock.

1. W = What You Want to Achieve

☐ You know what you want, why it's important, when and where you'll do it, and you have a vision board to remind you.

2. H = How to Do It

☐ You have your step-by-step route to your destination, your PLAN.

3. A = Accountability

☐ You've set up accountability and commitments with a partner.

4. C = Conditions and Structures

☐ You've set things up so it's easy for you to do what you need to do every day.

5. K = Kick-Start

☐ You know week by week what specific actions to take to achieve your goals.

If this is all clear, you can kick-start your project so you can take massive ACTION and bring your ideas to life.

THE UNSTOPPABLE 21 DAY CHALLENGE

STAGE 2

ACT

DOING YOUR 21 DAY CHALLENGE

STAGE 2: ACT

DOING YOUR 21 DAY CHALLENGE

"Victorious warriors win first and then go to war, while defeated warriors go to war first and then seek to win."

— Sun Tzu

You deserve a big round of applause because by getting this far, you have joined the 1% of the most productive people on the planet. You know what you want, you know how to get it, and you're ready to blast off.

One of the reasons the 21 Day Challenge is so effective is that instead of just hoping you'll somehow get things done, you've created a clear deadline to complete your project. This means you have opened an urgent window of opportunity within which you can give it all you've got, blast through Resistance, and claim your success—in 21 days or less.

You really have a lot of time to make things happen in 21 days. Each day of your 21 day challenge is priceless. Treat each day as if it was worth a billion dollars. Value yourself. Value your time. Value your life.

To help you stay on point and get the most out of each day of your challenge, I've included the following tips and techniques. Integrate them into your day and you'll find yourself feeling more energized and productive than usual.

ESSENTIAL PRODUCTIVITY TIP 1: YOUR DAILY IMPACT LIST

Simple as it may seem, the secret to taking massive, effective action every day is the The Daily Impact List.

You need to create a small list of your most important one, two, or three tasks for each day. Not any old list, not a BS list full of random stuff that wastes time, but a solid, highly effective 20% list with ONLY the most important things on it.

Many people have no idea what they are going to do each day and just drift along, attending to one crisis after another. Others have a list full of stuff that is mostly not effective. If you wake up and check your email first thing, you can be thrown instantly into a panic and waste the whole day chasing your tail.

What I'm suggesting is you have a simple list with only the most potent, impactful action steps on it and do those few things first each day before you do anything else. If you don't have this level of focus, failure abounds because once the distraction begins, it can be almost impossible to break out of it. By doing the most essential things first, you'll actually make real changes in your life in the next 21 days.

How to Create Your Daily Impact List

As you know, there is something magical about writing things down....

To create your 20% list:

1. Look at your week's results and actions
2. Pick one big result you want to achieve by the end of the day from that list
3. Write your big result on a small piece of paper every day

This means that before you begin your day, you have a clear, concise to do list of the most important things you need to do. By keeping that little piece of paper with you at all times, it will remind you of what's important and help you avoid distraction.

Trivial as it may seem, this is essential.

When I write down what I'm going to do each day, I do it. When I don't write my list, strange distractions begin to creep in. Without a clear, simple list, my day soon turns into a wayward adventure, doing anything and everything EXCEPT the things I need to do. Life is packed with distractions, so if we're not focused, it's possible to chew up entire weeks, months, and even years looking busy but getting nowhere. The distraction monster is hungry and highly active. Put it at bay with the clarity of your list.

I laugh at myself sometimes as I wander about the house, totally distracted, avoiding what is needed simply because it's not written down. Even if I know what to do in my head, I probably won't do it unless I write it down every day, or I'll do it at the last minute without full focus. After 20 years of working for myself, I still find that having this simple list makes a massive impact on my life.

Be warned! 21 days will be gone in a flash. Will you make your project happen? If you keep a solid list and do those things, you will! If not, chances are you'll fall back into old habits and miss out on this opportunity to achieve your dreams.

What's *Your* Big Upgrade Today?

What specific actions will you write on your highly productive 20% action list?

As you now know, not all actions are made equal. In fact, most stuff we do is simply low value distraction that does not move our life or work forward in a meaningful way. So, for you to get the most out of your 21 day challenge, aim to have ONE BIG SUCCESS towards your mission each day.

The delusion of time management is that everything you do is equal—that if you just write a list of all your actions and tick them off one at a time you'll end up successful.

The truth is only about 20% of your actions will lead to 80% of your results in any given day. That's why it's critical to focus on the handful of powerful actions each day that will give you the biggest bang for your buck and get them done first thing in the morning.

To make sure your daily list will get you big results, put only **one to three** highly effective actions on your list. It's tempting to cram our days with endless tasks but running around ticking off boxes all day is a sign of self-sabotage, not success.

Each day, there are only a handful of your most important actions that will have a long-lasting positive impact on your life and work.

So don't waste time on those pointless, long-winded to do lists that make only minor improvements to your goal. Just focus on the 20% that gets 80% of the impact. Often just one big upgrade or one main action is enough for the whole day. The fewer things on your list, the better. Don't try to do everything at once. Just focus on getting results that matter.

If you have a list of 3-5 things you need to do, focus on the most effective ones first when you have the most energy. Then do all your lower value tasks and administrative work later on in the day when you have less energy.

How to Assess Your Daily List

Your daily action list isn't just a list of random tasks. It's specifically designed to move you toward your destination one big, important step at a time. If the things on your list are not clearly creating results and moving you towards the achievement of your goal, something has gone wrong!

Take a good look at your main aim. What are the handful of things you need to do to achieve your goal?

Get clear on the one to three things that will create the most significant results and make them happen before you do anything else.

Write your list now. You'll feel awesome and you'll know exactly what to focus on.

Make Your List a Daily Ritual

I recommend you create your impact list every day, first thing in the morning before you do any work. Make sure it always consists of the top 20% of actions that create tangible impact and don't start work until you have a clear idea of the MOST IMPORTANT THING that you're wanting to achieve today.

At first you may not be clear how powerful the things you're doing are. But as the days go by, you'll become an expert at taking massive action. Each time you do this exercise, you'll discover what your top 20% actions really are, and you'll be better able to discern which ones are just a bunch of BS. This 80/20 thinking will change your life. You'll have more time, more money, more freedom, and more fun.

ESSENTIAL PRODUCTIVITY TIP 2: DESTROY DISTRACTIONS BEFORE THEY DESTROY YOU!

Even if you have an amazing vision, a solid plan, and an impact list that could knock out Mike Tyson in one punch, it's still not enough for you to actually do anything! We need to clear the clutter and distractions from our lives and make space for these new actions so we don't get pulled away from what's important and end up on a movie marathon, drinking binge, or some other alternate route that traps us in distraction.

This may seem obvious, but it is essential. If you want to knock it out and make things happen fast, it's critical to remove or massively reduce all distractions from your life. If you're surrounded with opportunities to distract yourself, you will get distracted.

Technology is a double-edged sword, a blessing and a curse. On one hand, we have truly incredible tools to get things done that have made our lives easier and allowed us to do things we'd never be able to do 10, 20, 50, or 100 years ago. On the other hand, these same devices are also the ultimate distraction traps because in just a few clicks we can access the web, mess about with apps, talk to people, and do an infinite number of other things that take us down the rabbit hole of distraction.

Modern smart phones have been purposely turned into virtual slot machines to keep us clicking, scrolling, and staring at our screens. The business model behind many companies is based on screen time. The more you look at their apps or websites, the more they get paid. This incentivizes companies and their evil genius app designers to create hopelessly addictive elements that prey on our human weaknesses and make it almost impossible to take a break from our phones. If you're interested in how distracting technology has become, you can learn more about it and discover ways to protect yourself at digitaldetox.io.

Be warned, all those notifications are designed to get you hooked. They provide an endless stream of new (potentially exciting) things for us to experience. And once we've become addicted to finding out what's new, we begin to feel we are missing out if we step away from technology for even a few hours. This modern addiction has created an ongoing sense of anxiety, restlessness, and inability to focus, making it harder and harder to actually get any quality work done.

The biggest problem is we often don't even realize what's happening. Procrastination happens mostly unconsciously. It has become so easy to fall into the endless phone-checking trap because it's a habit. We don't realize what we're doing until it's too late, and then hours have passed on social media or videos or texting or whatever. Before you know it, the day is over and not much has actually happened.

For example, yesterday I intended to finish this book. I worked from 5:00-6:30 a.m. Then I went to the beach for a walk and thought about what else needed doing to finish up. I got home and faithfully worked until about noon. So, all in all, it was a productive morning. But what happened next?

I intended to take a quick break for lunch and a nap before getting back to work. Instead, I found myself watching The Hobbit: An Unexpected Journey. Once that ended, I thought I may as well watch the sequel, The Hobbit: The Desolation of Smaug. Before I knew what happened, five hours had passed. That is some serious distraction. It wasn't until about halfway through the second movie, as the sun was setting, that I truly noticed what had happened and had a little giggle to myself about it.

Interestingly enough, it's not all bad. I did do a lot of work in the morning, and I'm back at it again now finishing up. Truth be told, it's not easy to be highly productive and focused all day long, so I was pushing it by trying to write after lunch at all.

Remember: The 80/20 principle explains we can't be effective all the time. It's simply not possible. We can increase our productivity by doing more of the effective 20% though, even if it's not possible to maintain that level of effectiveness all day long. I've tried to focus exclusively on the top 20% back to back to back, but it doesn't last. I've found the best I can do is triple the 20% so I'm spending 60% of my time doing highly effective work. More than that and it feels like I'm trying to bend time or live in another dimension.

So yes, I do get distracted and you will too. For me, the distraction normally comes later on in the day once I've already done the top things I need to do.

This story could have been a lot worse. Imagine what would have happened if I'd woken up and decided to watch a movie in the *morning* instead of writing. All my morning motivation would be wasted in entertainment and I'd end up feeling drained and defeated. If we're not careful, days and weeks can go by like that until the money runs out, or some other crisis comes our way to wake us up.

In our western culture, distraction is rampant. Most people are so swamped in distractions that they never get to the important things. There are many distractions to watch out for beyond watching TV, checking Facebook, and surfing the web. We can distract ourselves doing stuff that looks productive but in retrospect was a waste of time. In fact, I think most things we do are distractions from what's truly important. We live in a state of constantly being interrupted by cell phone alerts, emails, daily dramas, and other people. It seems as if our modern world has been designed to be an endless distraction from the moment we wake up until the moment we go to bed. If we are to get anything done, we need to focus on that top 20% and remove everything that can shake us up and knock us off track.

The 20-Minute Curse

Did you know that each time you are interrupted from a state of flow (when you're in the zone being focused and productive), it takes about 20 minutes to get back to the same level of focus you had before?

So if you're writing and someone calls you or texts you and you stop to look at your phone, it will take about 20 minutes to get back into the same level of productivity and focus you were in.

I don't know about you, but I don't want to waste all that extra time getting back in the zone. I don't want to live in a state of constant crisis, putting out fires, and being anxious. I'd rather get in the flow, do the work needed, and move on to the next thing so my life is enjoyable, successful, and actually works!

If you want to get things together, here are a few tips for removing distractions so you can focus and take care of the important things you need to do... and do them as quickly and easily as possible.

The Most Dangerous Distractions and How to Remove Them

CELL PHONE: The cell phone is a wonderful invention that holds enormous promise for productivity and joy—but it's also a double-edged sword. If I were the devil and I wanted to create the most potent tool to make people procrastinate and waste time, I'd invent the smartphone and make sure everyone had one. This magical device, like Frodo's ring in *Lord of the Rings,* is simply far too addictive and distracting for most of us to handle and use effectively. Most people have their phone with them at all times, fondling it regularly. Many even sleep with their phone at arm's length.

Over two billion people now do the smartphone prayer: bowing to look at their phone hundreds of times per day. The reason smartphones and other wireless mobile devices (WMDs) are so hard to put down is because they are purposely designed to be addictive. They are unlike any technology before them.

As Catherine Prince writes in the book *How to Break Up with Your Phone,*

> *"Steve Jobs was right: smartphones really are different. They're different in a lot of good ways, obviously. But smartphones also talk back at us. They nag us. They disturb us when we're working. They demand our attention and reward us when we give it to them. Smartphones engage in disruptive behaviors that have traditionally been performed only by extremely annoying people. What's more, they give us access to the entire internet. And, unlike previous technologies, we keep them near us at all times. Smartphones are also one of the first popular technologies to be specifically engineered to get us to spend time on them. In the words of Tristan Harris, a former Google product manager who's now working to raise awareness about how our devices are designed to manipulate us, 'Your telephone in the 1970s didn't have a thousand engineers on the other side of the telephone who were redesigning it to be more and more persuasive.'"*

The idea of leaving home without it these days seems almost dangerous and irresponsible, as if we now have a moral obligation to keep it with us at all times and be constantly available and connected to the world 24/7. With your smartphone, you can text, tweet, check your email, call people, receive calls, play with countless apps, and check social media. You can even watch full-length films all day on them. The possibilities for distraction and procrastination are endless.

If you want to get anything done, turn it off while you're working. It may sound crazy, but the world will continue without your phone being turned on. You could also turn it on airplane mode so no one can contact you while you work because getting text messages and phone calls will ruin your concentration and productivity.

If you just do this ONE thing, your ability to make things happen will drastically improve.

If you're one of the growing number of people who feel your phone is causing you a lot of harm and is too distracting, you may want to take it one step further and learn how to do a digital detox to claim back your time from the onslaught of digital distractions.

To find out more about how to do this, go to your free bonus resources and you'll find tools to support you and help you stay focused.

THE INTERNET: Ah, the internet, like the cell phone, is a marvelous creation and gives us access to almost anything we want to know in a matter of seconds. However, when you know what you need to do, ANYTHING EXCEPT DOING WHAT YOU NEED TO DO IS PROCRASTINATION.

I personally recommend you turn OFF the internet if you're not using it. I know it sounds a bit radical, but at every moment you are just one second away from being triggered and entering a trance where procrastination can consume you for minutes, hours, days, or weeks. Don't take the risk. Just turn it off. You can unplug your internet router or turn off the Wi-Fi on your computer. If you can't handle that, get an internet blocking app that stops you from going on distracting websites for a select period of time. Bottom line: remove the temptation to distract yourself, and you'll get far more good work done with a lot less stress. Make it easy for yourself to get your most important work done!

PEOPLE: Charles Dickens knew the score: He installed a second door in his office to block out noise, and no one was allowed to interrupt him while he was working. If he'd had a computer with access to the internet, a cell phone on his desk beeping at him, and worked in a busy office where he was being interrupted constantly, do you think he would still have managed to publish over a dozen major novels, a large number of short stories, a handful of plays, and several non-fiction books? I don't think so. In fact, we might never have heard of him at all.

People are awesome. But when you're focused on getting something finished, they can be a huge distraction. I've made a point to let everyone know that when I'm working, I am not available unless it's a REAL emergency that requires my attention. When I mean emergency, I'm not talking about the times a friend is about to get in line at the health food store and urgently wants to know if she should get an extra box of something for me and save the $1.72 or not. The answer is no. It's not important. When I say urgent, I'm talking about life threatening situations like an accident, tsunami, hurricane, or war.

If you want to get important work done, close the door. Lock it if you have to. Tell people you're not going to be available for an hour or two so you can FOCUS. When my wife goes away, I can get more work done in less time. She doesn't interrupt me that much, but just having her around is distracting. I love her dearly. And I also have to tell her, "When I'm writing, please don't interrupt me or talk to me until I'm done." Realistically, that question she has about something around the house can wait an hour and it won't make much difference, but if my work session is interrupted I won't be as productive. That means things won't get finished as quickly and my projects will drag out far longer than they need to. Those "quick" questions can end up wasting hours, days, weeks, and even years of our lives. It's better to focus on one thing at a time and then give the people in your life your full attention when you're not working.

If you simply remove these three distractions—cell phone, internet, and people—your ability to focus will instantly and automatically increase and you'll be amazed at how productive and successful you become.

ESSENTIAL PRODUCTIVITY TIP 3: THE MAGIC TIMER

Here's a final tip to instantly super-charge your focusing power and effortlessly breeze through the things on your list.

Use a timer at the beginning of each work session. Before you begin, select the amount of time you're going to work (for example, 50 minutes). When you're ready, hit START and work on your task until the timer goes off. Then you can have a break. When you're ready, hit start on the timer again, and do another work session. It may sound simple, but it's extremely helpful to overcome procrastination and get things done.

I'm not quite sure why this method is so incredibly effective, but for some reason turning on a timer to set a time to start and finish my task changes my mood in seconds. I go from mildly interested or even disinterested to being passionately determined, taking massive action and making things happen with bubbling enthusiasm.

For me, pressing start on my timer is like going from half dead and struggling to breathe to winning the Gold for a 100-meter sprint at the Olympics.

I tell you, a timer is magic. Here's what to do. **Get a timer.**

Options for Timers

PHONE: You can use your phone as a timer. But be warned: if you're tempted to check messages and play with it, then don't use it. Get another timer.

STANDALONE TIMER: You can buy standalone timers from kitchen shops or electronic shops.

POMODORO TIMERS AND APPS: You can get a Pomodoro timer app on your computer or use an app like Focus that blocks your internet connection and allows you to focus. There are countless timers online.

HOURGLASS: You could even get super old school and buy a sand timer. I've recently bought an hourglass that sits on my desk. When I'm ready to get started, I just turn it over and get to work. Watching the sand flow through gives a real feel for the passing of time. If you like the physical feeling of things in our overly digital work, you might like this. Try it.

Whatever kind of timer you use, it designates a time during which you will work and not be distracted. The main thing here is just to get a timer—any timer— and get moving. As long as it works, it's great!

Be Prepared to Focus

1. Remove your distractions so you can focus.

2. Look at your list and pick something. Either pick the one that's most important or if you can't figure out what to do, just pick any of them.

I'm assuming you have a list and the things on your list are truly important things, not time-wasting, pseudo-productive tasks that won't get you where you want to go.

If you don't have a clear list, go back and get one first before you move forward.

Set Your Work Times

There are many ways to work and it's important that you try different things out and discover what works best for you. After experimenting, I've discovered that I get the most quality work done by doing a 50 minute work session, taking a quick break, and then doing another 50-minute session. Then take a longer break.

My work time looks like this:

50 minutes super-focused work

10 minutes break (get a drink, walk about, go outside, lie down)

50 minutes super-focused work

30-60 minutes break (rest, relax, eat, go for a walk, etc., to get recharged and refreshed)

Then I do it all again.

50 minutes work

10 minutes break (get a drink, walk about, go outside, lie down)

50 minutes work

30-60 minutes break (rest, relax, eat, go for a walk, etc.)

If I want to do even more work, I do it all one more time. If you just do two sessions of 50-10-50 per day of high-value work, you'll be flying ahead and procrastination will be a thing of the past.

Some people who believe in the Pomodoro method say 25 minutes is a perfect amount of time to work before you take a break. Others like to work for 1.5-2 hours at a stretch. For me, the 50-10-50 does the trick. Discover whatever works best for you. Don't get too flustered about the numbers here. If in doubt, just work for an hour at a time. The main thing is to work while you have high energy and stay focused on the task at hand. Avoid social media, texting, and email by all means during your 21 day work sessions and breaks. Experiment with these methods and discover for yourself what works best for you.

Press Start and Do It

Finally, this is the bit that we've all been waiting for. This is where you actually DO the things you've been putting off and start getting your life back together.

By this point, you've removed almost every possible reason not to take action, so by the time you press the start button, you're truly ready to rock and roll and make things happen.

If you're anything like me, you'll find it's actually fun to have a deadline and see how much you can get done in your allotted time.

Once you hit START, just GO! Don't worry about being perfect. Don't worry about whether you're doing things exactly right, and don't get stuck second guessing yourself. Just start taking action on your most important task and keep working until the timer goes off. By doing this, you'll make huge progress on the specific tasks you've been putting off. More importantly, you're building the inner strength and habits to take action every day and make your dreams come true. It's like building a muscle. The more you use it, the stronger it gets.

Even if you get a little off track the way I did watching two movies back-to-back while I meant to be writing, you'll still be back at it the next morning, focused on making things happen.

I can't stress enough the power of consistent, daily practices like this. These new habits are what will save you from the wrath of procrastination and crisis. Every moment you invest doing this, you're breathing new life back into your dreams. You're taking charge of your reality and becoming the captain of your own ship, the master of your destiny. Is there anything more important?

A STINKY CORPSE AND A BROKEN TOE: A FUNNY STORY AND GENTLE WARNING ABOUT ACCOUNTABILITY

Can it really be easier to dig up a stinky dead corpse and break your toe than set up accountability? Yes.

In case you've been wondering what can happen when you set up your accountability, here's a real-life story that will make you chuckle....

One morning I noticed a disgusting stench wafting into the house making it hard to breathe. For a while I tried to ignore it, but it got worse and worse until I realized it was that foul stink of death from a rotting corpse. In Kauai, there are wild chickens that roam freely causing mischief. And when they die, the smell of their decaying bodies spreads like rotten wildfire.

Perhaps the dead chicken was symbolic of how much my own life had begun to stink and rot without my realizing it. As I complained about the smell, I suddenly awoke from a trance that had taken me over for many months. All of a sudden, I snapped out of it and realized that I'd long ago abandoned the accountability practices that had made such a profound improvement to my life.

After my initial successes, I'd become arrogant, complacent, and proud. Slowly, my life had unwittingly fallen into disarray. I was no longer doing the things I needed to do to feel awesome and be at the top of my game. I had begun to slack off into a mediocre existence. By abandoning my cherished daily practices, my life had become progressively more bland, boring, and depressing, and I wasn't happy about it. This was a new moment, and it was time to get my life back on track.

Spurred on by the fowl stench of rotting flesh, I made an empowering decision to reintroduce my accountability practices and get my life together again. I was going to make a commitment to implement 12 things I wanted to do each day to radically upgrade my life in one shot.

Unfortunately, it wasn't as easy as I thought. Here's what happened....

Full of excitement, I pulled out my Vision Files, a stack of papers in which I had already clearly articulated the *exact things* I needed to do to feel awesome. Next, I considered who I was going to set up my accountability with. I was just about to contact her with the details when I fell back into an unconscious trance to distract myself from this monumental act of freedom. The dead chicken stench had gone too far. Before I knew it, I'd abandoned my task and rushed out into the garden to locate the filthy corpse that had been insulting my nostrils. I grabbed a cardboard box and spade and into the jungle I went using my nose to guide me.

As I breathed death into my lungs, I realized how severe the Resistance was to setting up this accountability. Reeking like hell, with spade in hand, I laughed at how *I'd prefer to pick up a stinking, dead corpse than set up accountability!* I'd do almost anything to get out of it. If there wasn't a dead chicken, I'd probably have invented some other crisis to distract me or gotten lost with text messages, emails, movies, or some other nonsense to avoid what I needed to do.

Holding my nose and trying not to breathe, I negotiated the maggot infested corpse into the box and tossed the dead bird into the jungle. Feeling slightly nauseous, yet satisfied with myself, I wandered back inside to finish off what I'd started.

Before I knew it, I was once again putting off the inevitable and spacing out. This time my choice of distraction was watching a random video on Facebook. The video showed hotels in Las Vegas being demolished. How appropriate. It was the end of an old way of being and the beginning of another. Before the new life can be built, it seems the old one must first be leveled.

Rather than getting back on task, I noticed how hungry I was. I made myself lunch (see the procrastination at work here). After lunch, I took a nap, to recover my energy, of course....

Finally, I had the motivation to get to work and wrote a long list of all the specific things I needed to do and sent it to my new accountability partner to review. The deed was almost done! I had almost set myself up for massive success.

All that was left was to pick up the phone to call her and talk about it. I was just about to make the call, but before that could happen, I "accidentally" smashed my foot with full force directly into a concrete step, breaking the big toe of my left foot. The pain was so severe I had to laugh.

This was getting absurd. What next? I thought. Stab myself in the heart, fall off a cliff, get hit by a stray plane crashing into our house?

Literally seconds after breaking my foot, I picked up my phone and noticed it was 11:11 a.m. Classic. By this point, I had no choice but to pay attention to the outer expression of my inner Resistance. Unable to do anything else, I spent the next few hours bandaging my toe, lying down, and icing my foot to keep the swelling down. Finally, I did contact my friend and talked about our agreement and we got started. I had over 12 things I'd agreed to do each day, including getting up before 3:00 a.m. for meditation and doing extremely focused work for four hours per day.

Day one nothing much happened because I couldn't get out of bed and needed extra rest to recover from my injury. After a day of resting and healing, I was able to start my practices and take the big plunge to freedom (with a limp).

The story wasn't over yet. The next day, I officially started my accountability and felt great! Spurred on by my initial successes, I was even more excited to simplify and streamline my life. I noticed the one thing that was wasting my time and slowing me down was my cell phone.

While I was pondering what to do about my cell phone, I hobbled out to relax in a hotel. While I was out, I decided it was about time to put a password on my phone in case I lost it. Just as I entered the code, someone from the hotel came along to ask me a question and distracted me from what I was doing. Before I knew it, I'd entered a code into my phone that I couldn't remember. So now I was locked out of my phone!

After wasting a couple of hours researching how to regain access to my phone, I discovered the only solution to unlock the phone was to erase it completely which meant losing all my data, including videos, images, and everything else I had stored on the phone. So by the end of day one of my accountability, I had a brand new phone with no apps, no contacts, messages, or distractions. Not what I'd expected, but my subconscious mind got the result. The deeper part of me seemed to be at work here and I was watching it all in awe and wonder.

The next morning, day two of my new accountability, I woke up feeling great again. I noticed a slight irritation in my eyes and began to sneeze. I got up anyway and the symptoms continued as the day went on, gradually getting worse until it reached a point where I couldn't do anything. I looked in the mirror and saw my eyes were blood red, my nose was running like a waterfall, and I felt like a slimy beast. I coughed, spat, and spluttered about in agony, completely debilitated with a broken toe, literally unable to do anything except lie down and cough and splutter. The Resistance had kicked in again and totally knocked me out. So that was it! For the next few days, I simply couldn't do anything related to my accountability and even regressed back to a state in which I was worse off than I had been before I started.

Be warned: when you directly oppose your old habits in an extreme way, you're in for some Resistance. In my case, I tried to implement twelve habit changes at the same time, and it backfired severely.

There are two big takeaways from this story.

1. The Resistance Is a Sure Sign You're on the Right Path

Many people have been told, "If it doesn't feel good then it's bad." Sadly, this is not always true. Think about how many terrible choices have been made because they "felt good" in the moment but led to long-term problems. Checking email and going on social media may feel good, so may consuming drugs or distracting ourselves in countless ways instead of doing what we need to do.

Taking a mature attitude toward life means doing what's right even though it may be hard and not feel good at the moment. For example, I don't like doing yoga, but I feel good afterward. I don't always feel good when I start to work, but later on I'm happy I did it instead of watching cat videos on YouTube.

Here's the shocking truth: the more severe the Resistance the better it is. Counter-intuitive as it may be, more Resistance means more potential success. Most people fail in life simply because the Resistance gets the better of them. They choose the easy option but neglect the hard choices that will change their lives. If you'd rather pick up dead corpses and smash up your toe than set up accountability, it's a sure sign you're doing something significant and the old habits are afraid for their lives. Change means different, and different can be terrifying for us, even if it means we're going to have a massive upgrade. We live in a backward world where the things that are bad for us are extremely easy to do. Yet the things that are good for us are normally met with violent or unpleasant Resistance and drama. Get used to it and do it anyway, and success is yours.

2. Take It One Step at a Time

I've experimented with personal changes for over 20 years, and I've found that it's rare to be able to implement more than one new habit at a time with success. I'd like to think I can change multiple things at once, but I've been consistently humbled by my experiences. The maximum number of upgrades I've personally been able to sustain is three at a time, but it came with a higher level of Resistance.

Would you prefer a long line of failed attempts for success, or a gradual upgrade to your life where each month you're getting more and more effective and happy? Keep it simple. Implement one habit at a time and move on from there. Slow and steady at the beginning leads to extreme speed and power over time. Pick the one thing that matters most and you'll begin to see the proof in your results. Once you've successfully instilled a new habit into your life, add another, then another, and another. That's how you create a truly extraordinary life.

THE UNSTOPPABLE 21 DAY CHALLENGE

STAGE 3

RELAX!

CELEBRATE AND RENEW

CHAPTER 19

STAGE 3: RELAX!

PLAN YOUR POST-CHALLENGE BREAK TO REST, REJUVENATE, AND CELEBRATE

"People of our time are losing the power of celebration. Instead of celebrating we seek to be amused or entertained. Celebration is an active state, an act of expressing reverence or appreciation. To be entertained is a passive state—it is to receive pleasure afforded by an amusing act or a spectacle.... Celebration is a confrontation, giving attention to the transcendent meaning of one's actions."

— ABRAHAM JOSHUA HESCHEL

We all need to take time to relax, celebrate our success and feel renewed. As you know, the Unstoppable 21 Day Challenge has three stages to go to WAR with the Resistance and become unstoppable.

STAGE 1: WHACK – Win at the Beginning

STAGE 2: ACT – Do the 21 day Challenge

STAGE 3: RELAX – Celebrate and Rejuvenate

Now is the best time to get set up for stage three, RELAX, where you will take time off to relax and celebrate your success.

Get clear on stage three at the beginning because if you wait until the end of your 21 day challenge to figure out what to do, you'll probably end up not taking a break at all. The truth is a high-quality celebration and deeply renewing break requires some planning and foresight.

There is a big difference between coming up with a half-ass plan in the morning one day and carefully crafting a truly extraordinary vacation and life-enhancing, profoundly refreshing time off.

To really unplug and renew, you will probably need to block off your calendar so you can get away easily. You also may need to book tickets and get other things ready and packed, so by the time you finish your 21 day challenge you can take off and celebrate right away.

Imagine how great it would feel to finish your successful 21 day challenge and ride off into the sunset to celebrate your success and bask in your great new life. You can create that type of experience for yourself now with a little planning and creativity.

It's all too common for us mad creators to finish up one project, barely acknowledge our success, and without thinking, plunge straight into the next. This is bad news for a number of reasons. First, we all need a break. Without a break, we get burned out and our lives feel like an endless grind, a hamster on the treadmill with no end in sight. It's no fun, and we also end up less productive because without celebrations and time off, we can't be fired up and excited about life.

HOW TO TAKE A QUALITY BREAK

1. Choose something to do that will make you feel truly inspired, refreshed, and renewed.
2. Decide when you'll do it.
3. Block time on your calendar NOW to do it so you don't fill up your week with more stuff.

You don't need to take weeks or months away to feel refreshed. Many people find that even a three-day weekend is enough to feel wonderful, as long as it's planned right. Make your time off as long or short as works for you. The main thing is to fully embrace your time off and come back supercharged to create something else in your life.

As you craft your relaxation experiences, consider what activities and environments truly inspire you.

What types of experiences make you feel alive?

What situations or activities refresh and rejuvenate you the most?

What makes you feel genuinely renewed and fulfilled?

There is no one right answer to these questions. The only thing that matters is that you feel refreshed, relaxed, and inspired. Your time off may be as simple as unplugging the internet, putting the kettle on, and reading that book you've been wanting to read. Or going for a long walk in nature. Or booking a spa or meeting up in person with some friends you haven't seen for too long.

Don't overcomplicate it. Just think about what you love the most and let your celebrations come from your heart. Then create your plan to make your heart's wishes come true.

GET CLEAR ON THE MOST INSPIRING WAY FOR YOU TO CELEBRATE SUCCESS

- How will you celebrate your success?
- What will bring you the greatest joy?
- What type of celebration will be so enjoyable that it will inspire you to go the extra mile and finish your 21 day challenge mission even when you're having Resistance?
- How many days will you take off?
- Who will you be taking your break with? Or will you be going solo?

UPGRADE YOUR CELEBRATIONS

Once you've come up with some ideas consider the following:

- How could this experience be 10x more enjoyable?
- How could this be 10x easier to plan and prepare for?
- What else could I add to make it more meaningful?
- What could I remove to make it easier?

Once you're clear on relaxation and celebration, write it down and put it somewhere you can see it clearly.

You can even add some images of this to your vision board to remind you of what you're going to be doing to celebrate once your 21 day challenge is over.

MY RELAXATION AND CELEBRATION EXPERIENCE

I will celebrate my success and enjoy quality time off by _____

_____

I will be doing this on _____ (date)

I commit to this because _____

_____

To make sure I am prepared for this time off, I will _____

_____.

Take the time to get this right because by the end of your 21 day challenge you'll be ready for a well-earned break. The better you plan this now, the easier it will be to take time off and enjoy yourself.

You may not be doing anything too elaborate at first, but still plan it out now, block off your calendar, and get ready to relax, rejuvenate, and celebrate.

Success is yours if you plan it out.

Congratulations! You know what you want to achieve, you have the plan to make this happen, and you know all the steps you will take to go from where you are now to where you want to be. Now you also know how you'll celebrate after you've completed your 21 day challenge.

CHAPTER 20

OVERVIEW OF YOUR UNSTOPPABLE 21 DAY CHALLENGE

This chapter serves as a recap of the entire Unstoppable 21 Day Challenge so you know exactly where you're at and what to do. It's also the beginning of the workbook section where you can simply fill out the worksheets and get your first 21 Day Challenge completed.

There are three stages of the 21 Day Challenge, WHACK, ACT, and RELAX, that combined allow you to win the WAR against your negativity, excuses, and Resistance so you can bring your greatest gifts into the world.

STAGE 1:

W = WHACK! The pre-challenge set up—winning before you start.

Get clear on your 21 day challenge game plan, and win the battle before it's ever fought.

STAGE 2:

A = ACT! Get It Done! Doing the Unstoppable 21 Day Challenge

Take massive action for 21 days and bring your ideas to life.

STAGE 3:

R = RELAX! Celebrate and Renew

Your post-challenge break to rest, rejuvenate, celebrate, and prepare for your next mission.

These three stages combined give you the power to wage WAR with Resistance and win. Time and time again.

WHACK. ACT. RELAX.

PREPARE. WORK. CELEBRATE.

CLARIFY. CREATE. REJUVENATE.

These three stages of making things happen make you unstoppable. You can win the war against all the things that have held you back in the past.

Let's take a closer look at how it works.

STAGE 1: WHACK!
THE PRE-CHALLENGE SUCCESS SETUP—
WINNING BEFORE YOU BEGIN

"Every battle is won before it's ever fought."

— Sun Tzu

W = What Do You Want to Achieve in 21 Days?

Step 1: What Do You Want to Manifest?

Write down *all* the things that are unfinished and stressing you out. Just get them all out of your head and onto paper.

Step 2: Pick One Main Thing to Work on Now for the next 21 Days

In the next 21 days I want to finish _____

_____.

Step 3: Why?

Why is your life going to be better once you've done this thing?

How will you feel?

Why is this important for you?

What other benefits are there for you doing it?

What will happen if you DON'T do it?

How will your life be WORSE if you don't do it?

Who will you let down if you don't do it?

What negative things will you feel if you don't do it?

Complete the sentence:

This is important to me because _____
_____.

Step 4: When?

What's your end date?

When is the deadline for this thing you've picked?

Pick a specific day.

Write it down clearly. Give yourself enough time, but don't put it off too far or it will not have any power.

I will finish _____
_____by _____.

Step 5: Where and When?

Where will you do it?

It's all very well to have this written down, but where will you actually do it?

Complete this entire statement:

I commit to finishing _____

_____.

This is important to me because _____

_____.

When and where will I work on this:_____.

Step 6: Create Your Vision Board

Choose simple images that inspire you to make it happen.

H = How

Step 1: Write down What You Want

Get clear on where you're going.

Step 2: Write down the Best Plan You Can Think of to Get That Result.

For example: call Bill, set up an appointment. Meet with Susie. Finish the draft, etc.

This is your first route. Now, here's where it gets interesting.

Step 3. Look at Your Plan and Ask Yourself:

How could I do LESS work or take less time and get the same result?

How could my plan be at least four times faster and four times easier?

A = Absolute Accountability: The Magic Power to Make Anything Happen

Set up your bulletproof accountability (include who, what, where, and when to report).

Set up your 21 day accountability and your daily accountability.

C = Conditions for Your Success

What conditions and structures do you need to put in place for you to make things happen?

What do you need to add to your life? And what do you want to remove from your life?

Let's get clear on this right now.

Step 1: What Things Need to Be in Place to Make It Easy for You to Be Successful?

Remember, most of these conditions and structures are not difficult or complex things. In fact, if anything, they tend to look so simple that they seem to be barely worth considering. Don't be deceived by this simplicity. All that matters is that it works.

So what are your conditions and structures? Write them down.

Step 2: What Did You Miss?

Have another look. Are these conditions and structures going to guarantee your success?

Are they super easy? Are you clear on exactly what you need to do?

Write it all down so it's clear, and you can set it up easily.

What will happen if you do this?

Step 3: Do It NOW

Before you move on, go and set up those things. Buy whatever you need (your bananas and blender equivalent). Set up your life for success.

This is your key to freedom.

K = Kick-Start

Create your week by week plan. Identify the specific actions to take to achieve your goals and kick-start your 21 day challenge.

Complete your weekly action steps:

WEEK 1

RESULTS	ACTION
What do you want to achieve this week?	What actions will lead you to that result?

WEEK 2

RESULTS	ACTION
What do you want to achieve this week?	What actions will lead you to that result?

WEEK 3

RESULTS	ACTION
What do you want to achieve this week?	What actions will lead you to that result?

Now you just have to do it!

STAGE 2: ACT—DOING THE UNSTOPPABLE 21 DAY CHALLENGE

"Whatever you can do, or dream you can, begin it. Boldness has genius, magic, and power in it. Begin it now."

— GOETHE

21 Day Challenge Daily Routine

Each day of your 21 day challenge, follow these steps.

1. Get up early.

2. Look at your vision board, plan, and weekly action steps. Remind yourself of what you're doing, why you're doing it, and what you need to do to be successful.

3. Write Your Daily IMPACT list: What do you need to do today to win on your mission?

4. Do your top 20% most effective work each day as early in the day as possible.

5. Set a timer when you work so you can stay laser focused.

6. Take at least one to two hours OFF each day to rest and recharge so you feel good while you work.

7. Avoid or remove distractions. This is a war! (If you do get distracted, don't beat yourself up about it. Remember your vision and get back on the mission!)

8. Share your results with your accountability partner by the end of the day.

Recommended: Take Time off Each Week to Recharge

To remain highly productive, take one to two days a week off to rest and recharge. Doing this will help you do better work and stay focused. This may mean going out somewhere without a cell phone to enjoy yourself, clear your head, and regroup for the next week. Even though you'll be taking time away from doing the work, you'll get more done over your 21 day challenge if you make sure you feel refreshed.

Remove Distractions

As much as technology can help us be more productive, it can also completely cripple our productivity. If possible, block the internet and remove cell phones and WMDs while you're working so you can focus without interruption for longer periods of time. Implementing this one tip can be the difference between total success and total failure. You are an unstoppable get it done ninja! You know what to do!

STAGE 3: RELAX! TIME TO REST, REJUVENATE, AND CELEBRATE

My Relaxation and Celebration Experience

I will celebrate my success and enjoy quality time off by _____

_____

I will be doing this on _____ (date)

I commit to this because _____

_____

To make sure I am prepared for this time off, I will _____

_____.

You are a genius and you deserve a well-earned break and a wonderful celebration.

Now it's time to take time off to enjoy, renew, bask in your success and get ready for the next mission.

1. Get away to your special relaxation place.

2. Celebrate your success! Take at least a moment to truly appreciate yourself for the work you've done.

3. Relax, rest, and do things that genuinely renew and fulfill you.

4. Reflect on what you learned in the 21 day challenge and how you can do better next time.

Recommended

Get away into nature and unplug from all the endless distractions and notifications of modern life. You'll be amazed how good you feel when you're connected back to yourself, the real world around you, and no longer staring at a screen (I'm sure you've done enough of that already in your 21 day challenge).

Be honest about what you need to fully let go, relax, and renew, and give yourself the time and space to do it. The more renewed you feel, the happier you'll be and the more you'll have to give to others.

This is your "me time," so enjoy it fully.

WHAT'S NEXT?

Once you've completed your 21 day challenge and celebrated your success, you can repeat the process and started with your next 21 day challenge.

WHACK. ACT. RELAX. REPEAT.

Follow this process and success is yours.

> *"Follow your bliss. If you do follow your bliss, you put yourself on a kind of track that has been there all the while waiting for you, and the life you ought to be living is the one you are living. When you can see that, you begin to meet people who are in the field of your bliss, and they open the doors to you. I say, follow your bliss and don't be afraid, and doors will open where you didn't know they were going to be. If you follow your bliss, doors will open for you that wouldn't have opened for anyone else."*

— JOSEPH CAMPBELL

PART III

YOUR 21 DAY CHALLENGE

"To Embark on the Journey towards your Goals and Dreams requires Bravery. To Remain on that Path requires Courage. The Bridge that Merges the two is Commitment."

— DR. STEVE MARABOLI

CHAPTER 21

START YOUR OWN 21 DAY CHALLENGE

By now, you know exactly what to do and how to do it like an unstoppable ninja. The only thing left to do is get started! To make your 21 day challenge easy, we offer extra support so you can turn your ideas into practical results.

WHO QUALIFIES?

If you'd love to join our community of creators and be part of the Unstoppable 21 Day Challenge, your project or idea must meet the following criteria:

1. Aim for the Highest Good of All

This means your intention for bringing this idea to life is to create win/win situations that benefit everyone involved and make the world a better place.

2. Be Clear

If you're doing a project to help others, it's essential you are clear about WHO this is for and WHY it will help them. The more clear and focused your ideas are, the greater the results you will create.

Note: you can also do a 21 day challenge just for yourself, in which case just make sure you know exactly how it will help you and make your own life better.

3. Coming from Your Heart with Joy and Inspiration

Your idea brings you joy and is being created with a sense of happiness and genuine service to yourself and others.

4. You Really Care

You truly, honestly, and deeply care about who you are helping and about making your idea the best it can be. You're willing to go the extra mile to show your love and appreciation.

5. Ethical and Legal

Your idea is ethical and legal, meaning you won't get into trouble with the government by bringing this to life.

WHAT DO YOU GET WHEN YOU JOIN?

THE UNSTOPPABLE MASTERS PROGRAM (VALUE $350)

Your 21 Day Challenge Productivity Super Charge includes:

- A step-by-step video instruction guide on how to set up your 21 day challenge
- Powerful resources to explode your creativity and enable you to think more clearly
- Bonus methods to destroy Resistance and blocks for good
- Extra tools to double your productivity and help you get more done with less effort

Plus you'll also discover:

- How to take more time off, have more fun, and enjoy yourself (this is essential for you to be productive and have an enjoyable, meaningful life)
- How to celebrate your success and love your life
- Guided meditations to feel more relaxed, more creative, and think more clearly
- Additional recommended reading
- And a lot more

HOW TO START YOUR 21 DAY CHALLENGE WITH OUR COMMUNITY AND GET YOUR BONUSES

1. Enroll in your first 21 day challenge and get access to the bonus material. Go to:

    ## awakenedacademy.com/21daybonus

2. Study the bonus material and get acquainted with the website so you can get the most from all your bonuses and tools.

3. Set up Stage One: WHACK! Set yourself up for success and win at the beginning by filling in all the relevant documents and make sure you're all set and ready to rock to win before you start.

4. Ready? Then ACT! Blast off into Stage Two and get started on your Unstoppable 21 Day Challenge. There are bonus materials, support, and emails to help you make this easier and more fun.

5. All done? Relax! You deserve a break. Fully celebrate your success! Take a well-earned break and get ready for more.

6. Ready for your next mission? Repeat the process with a harder challenge and take your manifestation skills up to a new level. The more you do the 21 Day challenge, the more you'll create, and the greater your success in life will be.

7. Need more support and inspiration? Check out all the other bonus audios, videos, and tools to overcome Resistance and bring out the best of you.

HERE'S THE BASIC TEMPLATE FOR YOUR 21 DAY CHALLENGE

My Aim: What I Commit to Do in the Next 21 Days

I commit to _____

_____(completing what)

By _____ (date).

This is important to me because _____

_____ (why)

My Vision Board

I will create a simple vision board to remind of me of this challenge by putting

_____

_____ (what images?)

Where _____

(best place to see them so they remind you over and over again)

Daily Rituals for Success

For the next 21 Days I commit to doing:

1. _____

   _____ (your Work Success Ritual)

   at _____ (what time of day do you
   have the most focus and ability to get things done?)

2. And post what I did each day on Facebook (this holds you accountable
   by the group and helps you to keep on moving on!)

3. Optional: And_____
   (Your rejuvenation ritual—how will you feel awesome each day?)

Absolute Accountability: Make 100% Certain This Happens and Make Your Success Inevitable

Accountability for My 21 Day Results

If I fail to_____

(achieve my goals for this 21 day challenge)

by _____ (date)

I will (pay) _____ to _____ (whom)

This makes my success inevitable because _____

_____

(how will this guarantee you're successful?)

Accountability for My Daily Success Rituals

1. To make sure that each day I take massive action and move forward, if I fail to: _____

   (your success ritual)

2. And post what I did each day on Facebook (this holds you accountable by the group and helps you to keep on moving on!)

3. Optional: And _____

   (your daily rejuvenation ritual)

4. I will pay_____ (who) _____(how much per day)

5. This makes my success inevitable because _____

   _____

   (how will this guarantee you're successful?)

No-Wiggle Accountability

Starting _____ (date)

I will send _____ (who)

a _____ (text, email, call, letter)

to say _____

_____ (what you did — your daily rituals)

Failure to do this accountability or no communication = _____

_____ (consequence e.g., send $)

to _____ (whom)

I will stick 100% to my word and make sure I live up to these commitments because _____

_____ (why is this important to you?)

And I will do _____

_____

(how can you be 100% held accountable with no wiggle room?)

Bonus: Make It Easy With Success Structures

What little things can you do each day to make your life easy so you are surrounded with success?

1. _____ (Success Structure)

2. _____ (Success Structure)

3. _____ (Success Structure)

My Success Celebration After 21 Days

I will celebrate my success on _____ (date)

By doing _____

_____

_____ (what would bring you the most joy and create a meaningful completion to your 21 day challenge?)

Where _____ (where will you go?)

With _____ (with whom will you celebrate, if anyone?)

To download your weekly plan, daily plan, and additional 21 Day Challenge worksheets, go to:

awakenedacademy.com/21daybonus.

CHAPTER 22

BONUS PRODUCTIVITY NINJA TRICK

You can use procrastination to your advantage.

Why did I write this book? I wrote it because I was actually procrastinating on doing other things I needed to do. I couldn't handle doing my top 20% so I decided to write this book instead.

But before you yell out "Charlatan! Hypocrite!" I want to let you know that you can actually use procrastination to overcome procrastination. Here's how it works.

I have a long list of things I need to do, and that list includes writing various books. It's not easy to write a book. In fact, sometimes I just sit there gritting my teeth, feeling a restless urge to consume some entertainment or escape my task at hand. If I intend to do something else that I don't want to do, then I can use the idea of writing a book as an excuse not to do it, which gets my ego onboard to helping me do something productive. And lo and behold, a book is written.

In other words, whenever we're doing the hard stuff that we need to do, we'll have Resistance and a desire to escape it. So, instead of wasting time watching TV or playing with your feet, use that energy to do something else productive that wasn't on your list. I already wanted to write this book, but I would not have finished it if it weren't for using procrastination to my advantage.

This ninja trick only works if you already have a clear list of important things you want to do but haven't had time for yet. It won't work if, instead of finishing your project, you decide to do a Harry Potter marathon and watch the entire series of movies back to back.

Part of creating a system that works for you and your life is knowing when to follow the system, when to make adjustments, and when to follow your intuition.

Life isn't about forcing ourselves into rigid systems. Systems are here to help us have a better life. So always keep in mind what your life is all about and what you want. Have the end goal in mind and don't lose track of what's truly important to you, or you may end up a slave to your own creations. You're not here to be a slave to ideas, beliefs, or lifestyles. Design this system to work for you.

Be the master of your creations.

I'll leave you with this to think about:

Who are you?

Why are you here?

How can you enjoy every moment of your life to the fullest?

I hope this was helpful. Many blessings and love.

CHAPTER 23

FINAL THOUGHTS

"How we spend our days is, of course, how we spend our lives."

— Annie Dillard

At the end of your life, what will matter most is that you enjoyed a life well lived. You did the things that mattered most to you and lived your own life and became who you were born to be.

I hope you enjoyed this book, and most of all I hope you use these methods to focus your energy on the handful of things that matter most to you—and claim back your life from the tyranny of distraction that can suck all your time away.

I'm the first to admit that living each day to the fullest is not easy. But then again, living in the shadow of our potential and playing small isn't easy either. It hurts us every day. So we may as well discover how to enjoy our lives to the fullest and embrace our potential however we can.

Many people ask me what the essence of these teachings is. What are the key things to remember?

There are just two things to focus on. If you do both of these success is yours.

1. CREATE DAILY RITUALS TO TAKE CARE OF YOURSELF

Your daily ritual is the most important thing you have to keep you on track. It includes the thoughts and actions you take each day to feel refreshed, happy, liberated, and alive. Because if you feel alive, then you'll be excited to live your life, share your gifts, and create wonderful things in the world.

What this means in practice is making sure you have some daily practices (even when you're taking time off) that empower and inspire you. Everyone is different and what works for one person may not work for you. Stay true to yourself and keep refining your daily rituals so your life feels as if it's your own and you are inspired to wake up and be alive. For some it may mean getting up early for meditation and yoga. For others, it's waking up with a hot cup of coffee and watching the sunrise with a book. Others enjoy taking a run.

Your daily rituals can be simple or more elaborate. The key thing is they make you come alive and feel good. If you do this every day, the rest of your life will feel more inspiring and enjoyable. So if you ever feel something is "off," get your daily rituals right and the rest will follow.

By the way, this also means there will be times when the best thing to do is nothing. Sometimes, we just need to take a break and get away from it all. I recently took a six-week break to just relax, connect with friends and family, meditate, and get more sleep. It was wonderful and inspired me to go to the next level in my work. If you feel you've been working too hard, then give yourself permission to stop and regroup. It will pay off in the long run. Working all the time is not the purpose of our lives. Quality work comes from inspiration and that inspiration is lacking if all we do is work. The secret to life is getting the right balance of self-service and service of others. If you need a break, take it. You'll soon be back at it and on your mission again.

2. CREATE SOMETHING EVERY DAY

Once you feel refreshed and inspired, you will naturally want to create and share. You have great work to do in your life. You are a creative being, and when you're sharing your gifts, honing your skills, and mastering your craft in service of others, your life has meaning. The handful of high-level skills that make the biggest difference are where you can create the greatest value.

The problem is the endless distractions that can eat up all your time and bury your special gifts in a corner. That's a terrible waste. Your mission is to know exactly what the most high-value skills and tasks are and focus on those things every day when you're fully energized and can give 100% of yourself to the task. Whatever you need to do to cut back the distractions so you can focus, do it.

We all need you to share your best and shine on. Aim to spend at least two hours a day doing your most high-value work and keep increasing that time until you spend all your most valuable working energy exclusively doing the things that matter most. If you do this, you'll find yourself producing 2-16 times more value each year and feeling more alive than ever before.

Conclusion

So there it is.

Focus on taking care of yourself so you feel alive and then jump in full blast to create your great work in the world. If you only do these two things every day, you'll find your life will be filled with more happiness, meaning, and inspiration. You'll wake up with purpose and go to sleep feeling contented and satisfied.

The 21 Day Challenge is a fun way to organize your time and your life so you stay focused on what matters most for you. Now that you have the method, feel free to refine and amend it to suit your needs and schedule. Make it work for you. Own it for yourself.

Wishing you a blessed life. Thank you for being here. Enjoy the journey.

Michael

ACKNOWLEDGEMENTS

Nothing happens in isolation. All great ideas are built on the foundation of what came before. This book would not have been what is it without the following influences.

First and foremost I share my gratitude to the One who gets things done through others. The spiritual teachings and meditation practices I've learned over the years have allowed wonders to emerge through me and for that I am truly grateful. Many of these can be found for free on our websites.

To all those who have faced their demons and done it anyway, I admire and respect you.

To Steven Pressfield, Joseph Campbell, Eben Pagan, Dan S. Kennedy, Richard Koch, Dan Sullivan, Joe Polish, Jim Loehr, and Tony Schwartz, among others, thank you for your inspiration and insights on getting things done and staying focused.

To Tom Corson-Knowles and the TCK Publishing team—Sarah Dyck, Jennifer Crosswhite, Ana Cristina Ochoa, and Queenie Faigones.

To Arielle, for your love, support and the ideas you shared.

To everyone else who has supported me over the years in various ways on my own creative journey. You know who you are.

Big love,

Michael

ABOUT THE AUTHOR

Michael Mackintosh is an internationally renowned author, spiritual teacher, entrepreneur, and mentor. He supports next-generation leaders and coaches as they reawaken their vision, unlock their genius, and systematically transform ideas into tangible impact, income, and freedom—while enjoying the journey and staying in the now.

Michael believes that future success need not be at the expense of well-being and a beautiful life today. His teachings promote living in the present, being connected to a Higher Power and Higher Purpose, and creating from a place of fullness, instead of chasing the dream while suffering in the moment.

At age 18, Michael had a profound, unexpected spiritual awakening that completely transformed his life and propelled him into a higher state of consciousness. This new, awakened consciousness and perspective gave him profound insights into the nature of Reality and what was possible in life.

Within a month of this spiritual awakening, Michael abandoned the ordinary world for seven years and went on a deep spiritual adventure into higher states of consciousness, traveling frequently to India to spend time with some renowned spiritual teachers and tasting the highest states of peace, freedom, and deep contentment.

The Journey Back

Emerging from his spiritual practice with visions and a passion to serve, he cofounded multiple successful companies serving countless souls all over the globe including: **Awakened Academy**, **Superhero Training** and **OmBar Chocolate**, among others.

Michael is known for his unique and refreshing clarity. He simplifies complex and often intangible ideas into clear, tangible insights that have empowered thousands to awaken to who they truly are, free themselves from limiting beliefs, and embrace their true dharma.

He is one of the only teachers who embraces both the spiritual and the material aspects of life and helps others experience both inner and outer abundance.

Having realized that there is nowhere to go and nothing to escape from, Michael discovered that the only path to true freedom was to "master being alive" and create the highest experience possible in the inner and outer worlds (which are intimately connected).

Michael reminds us that as we abandon trying to be someone else and focus on being our best self, we open up to receive nourishment from the Source, the only true, everlasting power.

He knows each soul has a unique mission and deep connection with the ONE, and it is only by maintaining that eternal, spiritual connection and living in alignment with the immutable laws of the universe that we can experience true awakened living.

He lives in between Sedona, Arizona and Kauai, Hawaii with his wife, Arielle.

OTHER BOOKS BY THE AUTHOR

For a complete list of all Michael's books go to:
michaelmackintosh.com/all-books

MORE BONUS GIFTS

For a variety of other free gifts, audios,
videos, free reports, and mini-courses go to:
michaelmackintosh.com/gifts

GET BOOK DISCOUNTS AND DEALS

Get discounts and special deals on our bestselling books at
www.TCKPublishing.com/bookdeals

28432852R00117

Made in the USA
Columbia, SC
11 October 2018